baguettes and bicycles

by

Steven Herrick

Table of Contents

About the author
Introduction – a cycle back to childhood
PART ONE: CYCLING ACROSS FRANCE
Chapter One – Saint Nazaire to Nantes
Chapter Two – Nantes to Le-Mesnil-en-Vallee
Chapter Three – Le-Mesnil-en-Vallee to Angers
Chapter Four – Angers to Savigny-en-Veron
Chapter Five – Savigny-en-Veron to Rochecorbon
Chapter Six – Rochecorbon to Chaumont-sur-Loire
Chapter Seven – Chaumont-sur-Loire to Orleans
Chapter Eight – Orleans to St-Firmin-sur-Loire
Chapter Nine – St-Firmin-sur-Loire to Pouilly-sur-Loire
Chapter Ten – Pouilly-sur-Loire to Decize
Chapter Eleven – Decize to Paray-le-Monial
Chapter Twelve – Paray-le-Monial to Beaune
Chapter Thirteen – Beaune to Rochefort-sur-Nenon
Chapter Fourteen – Rochefort-sur-Nenon to Besancon
Chapter Fifteen – Besancon to Montbelliard
Chapter Sixteen – Montbelliard to Mulhouse
Chapter Seventeen – Mulhouse to Basle

PART TWO: CYCLING UP FRANCE
Chapter Eighteen– a boy and a hill
Chapter Nineteen – A coffee in Paris
Chapter Twenty – Col de la Croix de Homme Mort
Chapter Twenty-one – Col d'Oeillon
Chapter Twenty-two – Mont Ventoux
Chapter Twenty-three - Mont Ventoux on a Sunday
Chapter Twenty-four – Alpe d'Huez
Chapter Twenty-five – Col de la Croix de Fer
Chapter Twenty-six– Les Balcons d'Auris and Col de Sarenne
Chapter Twenty-seven – Col du Glandon
Chapter Twenty-eight – Col du Galibier
Chapter Twenty-nine - lunch in a French restaurant

About the author

Steven Herrick is the author of twenty-one books for children and young adults. In Australia, his books have won the New South Wales Premier's Literary Award in 2000 and 2005, and have been shortlisted for the prestigious Children's Book Council of Australia Book of the Year Awards on six occasions. He is published in the USA by Simon and Schuster and Boyds Mill Press. He has also been published in the UK and The Netherlands.

Steven has written travel articles and features for newspapers and magazines and regularly travels the world performing his poetry and giving author talks in schools. He lives in the Blue Mountains in Australia with his wife, Cathie, a bellydance teacher. They have two adult sons, Jack and Joe.

www.stevenherrick.com.au

dothebikething.blogspot.com.au

Introduction

a cycle back to childhood

In 2010, my wife and I returned home to Australia after a few months in Europe. I weighed eighty-five kilos, more than I had ever done in my fifty-one years plonking around the planet. I stood in front of the bathroom mirror and turned sideways. The result of sixteen weeks of consuming European cakes, soft cheeses and pasta stared back at me.

It was late winter in the Blue Mountains, the wind whistled outside threatening to freeze-dry the cedar tree near our driveway. I sighed heavily. Everything I did, I did heavily. Pulling on baggy trackpants, a t-shirt, a polartec sweater and a rainjacket, I topped off the fetching ensemble with a knitted beanie. I was about to go cycling for the first time in many years. It was five degrees celsius outdoors. My wife shook her head, suggesting I wait until Spring. I answered that I'd weigh one hundred kilos by then. I walked out the door and into the tempest. In the backyard shed was my little-used Trek Mountain Bike, fortunately equipped with lots of gears. I'd need them all.

We live on a spur of land called Narrow Neck that juts into the Blue Mountains National Park separating two valleys. Sandstone cliffs and eucalyptus forests entice daytrippers from Sydney, one hundred kilometres east, to walk in the fresh mountain air. Busloads of Asian tourists pull up at the local landmark, the Three Sisters, a trio of time-worn rocks that present the perfect photo opportunity against the curious blue haze of the valley below. Tour guides explain the blue comes from the oil of the eucalyptus trees and the altitude.

I pump up the gnarly tyres of the Trek, tighten the seat adjustment and strap on my son's helmet. I am going cycling. A few months earlier in Italy, I had regularly seen old men cycling road bikes up and down the hills of Tuscany. If they could do it...

The wind predominantly blows from the west up here. I cycled east, downhill for a kilometre, grinning with the icy chill. And then I hit my first hill. Rapidly changing down to granny gear, I pedalled like a furious hamster, trapped in his wheel. The hill seemed to go on forever. My breathing became shallow and forced. I wondered if many of those Italian cyclists had heart attacks? Even though it was freezing, drops of sweat pinged on my handlebars. The odometer told me I'd ridden all of three kilometres. I struggled to the top of the hill and wobbled drunkenly across the road.

Another downhill. Followed by a long slow uphill. If I wanted to get fit, this was my future in the Blue Mountains. Mountains, by definition, mean there is very little flat land. I gloried in the five hundred metres of plateau before cruising down a long sweeping corner to Leura Cascades where a picture-perfect waterfall plunged into the valley. No time for sight-seeing though. I had another hill to climb, another heart attack to avoid.

That first day, I completed a paltry ten kilometre circuit. When I dismounted in our driveway, I dry-retched under the cedar tree. My marshmallow legs wobbled in time with my stomach as I returned the bike to the shed. I patted the seat. 'Tomorrow,' I said, hoarsely.

My wife greeted me at the door and made me an espresso, as if my heart needed more adrenaline?

The next day I was back at it. This time, twelve kilometres. Over the next month, I slowly increased my distance until one day I rode to the bike shop three suburbs away. I couldn't resist entering. The owner seemed surprised that anyone would be out cycling in this weather while wearing such inappropriate clothing. I bought my first pair of lycra shorts and leggings, blushing into the change-room mirror. I was going out in public dressed like that? Hanging from the far wall of the shop, I spied a fetching red hybrid bike with twenty-one gears and road tyres, much more suited to the cycling I was doing. I asked how much? Cheaper than medical insurance. The next weekend, I bought it.

A year later, after riding nearly eight thousand kilometres around my mountain neighbourhood, no matter what the weather, I was a confirmed cycling nutter. I wore lycra shorts and a lurid lime-green cycling jersey. I'd even bought a proper helmet. Occasionally, I took my new red hybrid on longer journeys, cycling eighty kilometres in a day, up and down, my breathing finally under some control. I began trawling the internet for routes to cycle, for biking holidays. I even started looking at road bikes. Racing bikes, we called them when I was a child. I pictured a (not-so-fat) old man on one of those? My wife, encouraging as always, wanted me to splurge on a carbon-fibre dream.

My local bike shop owner suggested a Specialized Roubaix road bike, carbon-fibre, compact gearing, with a long-distance race dynamic. He whispered the price. I told him I'd consult my wife, just once more. Her answer was to send me into the bathroom to stand on the scales. I weighed seventy-five kilos. I'd lost ten kilos in a year of happy cycling. I no longer dry-retched after a ride. I had even begun buying books on Tour de France mountains. I figured I cycled up mountains every day, why not, literally, aim high.

My wife told me to buy the bike. I always do as she says.

In the following year, I cycled another ten thousand kilometres, both in the mountains and occasionally further afield. I am a writer of books for children and young adults. My work takes me into schools all over the world. For the next year, whenever I travelled in Australia, I'd take my Roubaix, indulging in a cycle after school, just like I did when I was twelve years old. I had rediscovered my childhood, with the help of a bicycle.

I was on the way to discovering a hunger for adventure.

PART ONE

cycling across France

Chapter One

Saint Nazaire to Nantes

I'm in Saint Nazaire, a seaport at the mouth of the Loire River on the Atlantic Coast of France. It took thirty-four hours to get here, including two bum-numbing plane trips and two mercifully shorter train journeys. I arrive on a lovely spring afternoon and immediately put my hybrid bike together to go for a cycle. Sure enough, there's a shared bike path and promenade along the water. Every few hundred metres, a kiosk is open, offering beer, coffee and deckchairs to catch the last of the afternoon sun. The locals are out in force, especially the cyclists. And not one of them is wearing a helmet. Old men, children, sporty lycra-clad racers, teenagers, all sans safety gear. I feel like a man wearing flannelette at a fashion show.

I stop at a kiosk and dismount from the bike, my leg banging on the top of the panniers as I stumble towards the bar. I'm not drunk, just clumsy. Ordering a beer, I remove my helmet, recline in a deckchair and watch the cargo ships rolling in from the ocean, heading for the port around the bend on the Loire. It's a relief to not feel the rumble of jet engines under my feet, to be stationary.

Two motorcyclists roar into the car park behind the kiosk. They dismount without falling over and nonchalantly walk to the stripey-coloured deckchairs in front of me and order two beers. They take off their leather jackets to reveal blindingly white forearms. It's early May. I now have a view of my red bicycle; a dozen fishing boats bobbing in the harbour; a curious triffid-like crane that lifts the seafood catch from the fishing boats; and two overweight pale motorcyclists with unruly beards, tattoos and greasy stains on their jeans.

A Muslim woman wearing the veil calls to her daughter, dressed in pink, to wheel her stroller to the bench seat. The stroller is also bright pink. The daughter skips as she approaches her mother.

Families stroll along the promenade; an old man smokes alone on a foldaway chair; two teenagers flirt on the steps leading down to the harbour and I slowly overcome jetlag.

Saint Nazaire has a few old buildings, but the majority were bombed to rubble by the Allies in World War Two, for this town was an important Nazi U-Boat base. In fact, the remnants of the naval base still remain. Legend has it the concrete walls and roof the Nazis constructed were so thick, that demolition after the war proved impractical. So, making a positive out of a negative, the hulking monstrosity of a building was refurbished with cafes and restaurants. It's in a perfect location on the water, but nothing can hide the toad-ugliness of all that concrete. Imagine a bomb shelter six storeys above ground. Thankfully, they haven't tried painting it, or rendering - this is not Tuscany - it's a sombre reminder of what this pretty little town went through in the war.

After downing my beer, I brave the scorn of fellow cyclists and don my helmet once again, to go looking for the historic railway station, now reputedly undergoing renovation into an art centre and theatre. I find it soon enough, surrounded by a temporary builder's fence, which prevents me from getting close enough to see whether it still has the original glass ceiling. I suspect not. A pity. Because one of the great survival stories of World War Two happened here.

On a January night in 1943, the Allies flew one of many bombing raids over Saint Nazaire. One of the US planes was hit by German gunfire and broke apart at 6,000 metres. Staff Sergeant Alan Magee was thrown from the plane, losing consciousness as he fell to a certain death. Miraculously, Sergeant Magee landed on the glass ceiling of the railway station, which somehow cushioned his fall to the platform below, allowing him to survive against all the odds. He received numerous shrapnel wounds and several broken bones. The German doctors, perhaps sympathetic to his good fortune at surviving, patched up his extensive wounds and Magee spent the rest of the conflict as a prisoner of war. He returned to Saint Nazaire in peacetime to unveil a memorial to the airmen who lost their lives in fighting over the town.

I want to stand on the old railway platform and stare up at the glass ceiling, wondering what it must be like to fall from such a height, but it is not to be. I cycle around the theatre twice, in honour of Sergeant Magee and slowly make my way back to the centre of town. The light is fading and it's time for dinner.

My hotel room is in the main street of town. I love small-town French hotels. Simple, basic accommodation with double-glazing on the windows, a clunky grilled panel heater in the corner for warmth and those weird long cylindrical pillows that only a Frenchman could design. All this for the princely sum of 45 Euros! Breakfast of juice, croissant, baguette, jam and coffee is E6.50 extra.

It's Monday night in Saint Nazaire. The only restaurants open speak loudly to the multicultural Fifth Republic. A Turkish cafe, two pizza restaurants and a Chinese take-away are my choice within walking distance. I opt for a calzone, superbly cooked, loaded with champignons and jambon in the restaurant downstairs from my hotel. The friendly waitress brings me a carafe of rosé. Two single elderly French people are the only other diners. We have all ordered rosé. We smile at each other as the smell of pizza wafts from the kitchen. In celebration of my arrival, I daydream that the French yesterday elected their first socialist President in seventeen years, just for me. Bonjour Monsieur Hollande.

Tomorrow, I begin my cycle across France, west to east, following the Eurovelo 6 cycle path as it merrily wanders along the Loire River, before following a few canals, the Saone and Doubs Rivers and then linking with the Canal du Rhone au Rhin. It's signposted, sometimes. Therein, lies the adventure.

Starting in the seaport of Saint Nazaire, I hope to make it to Basle, Switzerland in eighteen days. Cycling the width of France is but a taster for what lies ahead. After Basle, I plan to journey by car, bike in the back, to the French Alps to ride up as many Tour de France mountains as I can find or as my fifty-three-year-old legs can tolerate. And, finally, if that doesn't kill me, an attempt on Mont Ventoux, perhaps the most iconic of Tour de France mountains, rising out of the Provence landscape of vineyards and olive groves.

But first, the width... the girth of France.

All this is dependent on my bike holding together. After two hours this afternoon, it's already creaking at the weight it's forced to carry. Two panniers and a middle-aged man who intends to stop at a boulangerie morning and afternoon. And, really, is a three course lunch acceptable, even in France? Followed by three courses for dinner. I plan on salade de chevre chaud, steak and frites, chocolate mousse... and then back on the bike. The creaking will only get louder.

The morning ride away from Saint Nazaire is cold and misty. An Atlantic squall swept in from the ocean as I slept and the streets are still shiny with rain. The Eurovelo is supposed to follow the Loire, but in the first hour, all I see is farmland and oil refineries in the distance, where I know the river must be. I am lost, a few kilometres into my trek. No matter. I have yet to see another vehicle on the road and my only companions are hundreds of birds singing just for me.

I crest a small hill and out of the mist comes a peloton of cyclists, heads down, legs pumping. I wave. One deigns to nod in response. I watch them disappear into the miasma. The birds keep singing. The river must be around here somewhere? I consult the map, again. Perhaps a cake will take my mind off this predicament? At least, I'm still heading east. I think.

In Donges, I stride purposefully into the boulangerie and point at the elegant row of cafe éclairs. Using my best garbled French, I ask for one. The young woman puts two into a petit cardboard container and begins wrapping it. 'Non, pardonne, une.' I bleat. She unwraps the treat and returns one éclair to the display. I elaborately mime that I plan to eat the éclair immediately, so she won't have to go through the wrapping all over again. The French love their cakes so much, they gift wrap morning tea. She shrugs and hands it across the counter with a napkin. I sit on the steps of the church in the square, the weak sun struggling through the clouds, and scoff my éclair. It's delicious, worth the decoration of wrapping.

The D17 is a very quiet road as I cycle past farmhouses and paddocks dotted with cattle. In one field, a dairy cow stands on a mound of dirt, staring at her companions circling. It's a cow-version of 'I'm king of the castle'. I'm tempted to wait and watch if the other cows attempt to storm the high ground. One bellows into the morning. I ride on, still searching for the Loire. At Saint-Etienne-de-Montluc, I make a decision to cycle due south, certain the river has to be there... somewhere. The road winds back on itself and I appear to be returning to Saint Nazaire. On my first day, I may have to board a train to traverse the sixty kilometres to Nantes. On the outskirts of Coueron, I enter the only open shop, a pizza bar.

'Parlez-vous anglais?' I ask, hopefully. Three 'nons' and a resigned shake of the head in response. I swallow, manfully, and blurt, 'Ou est Nantes?' pointing in the direction I expect to ride. The young African-French woman smiles and leads me out of the shop. She points in the opposite direction to where I was intending to cycle and says, 'Nantes.' She waves as I cycle away.

The next ten kilometres are spent on a suburban road with no bike lane and lunchtime buses ferrying people home for two hours of eating and siesta. Very civilised. At last, I see a sign for Nantes. I cycle around a corner and voila, there is the Loire. My first sighting in... check of Garmin... sixty-five kilometres. It's wide and brown and flowing fast towards Saint Nazaire and the Atlantic. A bike path threads between the river and the highway, past factories and shops and a battleship.

A what?

Yep, Nantes has it's own ship, on display for children and their parents to wander aboard and play sailors. You have to love a town that has a battleship moored opposite the art gallery. You can imagine the Admiral, let's call him Napoleon shall we, turning the guns on the museum cafe and threatening, 'Anyone who mentions Jean-Paul Sartre gets it!'

I bypass the free ship inspection and ride in ever-widening circles around Nantes. In 2004, it was voted Europe's most liveable city. Perhaps because every road has a bike lane? A happy city is a cycling city. On my travels, I find an impressive chateau with muscular fortifications and a cute little moat. Who'd attack a Chateau with a moat, the ducks gliding silently in circles. I also visit three stunning churches, occupying the high ground with impressive views to the Loire. Each one has the austere silence I so love of French cathedrals. I sit on a wicker chair in Nantes Cathedral and gaze at the ceiling, at the stained glass windows and the altar with Christ forever watching over his flock.

But what I really want to find in Nantes is a bike shop.

One day. One puncture.

Most shops are inexplicably closed. A man in the Place Royaïe, with immaculately shined shoes and the demeanour of an Accounts Manager on his day off, explains that today is a Bank Holiday. No wonder I had such quiet roads this morning. Just when I'm about to give up the search and look for an afternoon boulangerie instead, I spy a multi-storey sports store. The bike section is at the rear of the second floor. Along one wall is a shelf of bike tubes. If only they had my size in stock. C'est la vie. I buy an undersized tube, just in case. No need to worry, I won't get another puncture.

My bicycle and I take the train back to Saint Nazaire. Why? Because in my meticulous planning for this trip, I had bargained on plane delays, train derailments, hurricanes over the Indian Ocean, or simply falling asleep at Singapore Airport and missing my connecting flight. I expected to arrive a day late. So, I booked the same hotel in Saint Nazaire for two nights. As it was, the Singapore Airlines flights were on time, the French trains were efficient and comfortable, the hurricanes huffed and puffed and blew elsewhere and I did not fall asleep.

Tonight, I renew my acquaintance with a calzone and a pichet de rosé before retiring to my room and falling asleep almost immediately, dribbling elegantly on the French pillow. Tomorrow, I catch a commuter train back to Nantes and begin again. Too much planning is... too much planning.

Accommodation: Hotel De Touraine, Ave De La Republique, Saint Nazaire. E45 single. Breakfast E6.50. Friendly hosts, garden to park the bike, wi-fi that works, standard clean comfortable hotel room. My score: 14/20.

Route Tips: The official map suggests starting the trip in St-Brevin-les-Pins, on the south side of the Loire. That's fine, as long as you can cross the Pont de Saint Nazaire by bike. It's steep, windy, traffic-heavy and dangerous. Avoid it at all costs. If starting from Saint Nazaire, where the train station is, I'd suggest wandering the backroads on the north side until Coueron, where there is a ferry. Or stay northside until rejoining the Eurovelo at Nantes. The back roads are quiet and well-surfaced. French drivers are generally considerate of cyclists.

Distance cycled today: 78km

Actual Distance: 60km (this is the distance you'd cycle without detours and without getting lost)

What I should have said today: 'Yes, I will have that second éclair, for my friend Gustav, waiting outside on his tricycle.'

Chapter Two

Nantes to Le-Mesnil-en-Vallee

The commuter train to Nantes is crowded with elegantly dressed women in long overcoats and high heels, men in suits and serious reading glasses and one apologetic cyclist taking up too much space. Mercifully, the Eurovelo path is a stone's throw from Gare de Nantes.

Five kilometres into my ride this morning, on a hard dirt section of the Eurovelo 6, I get another puncture. Actually, my stupid ******* bike gets the puncture. I repair it with a very thin, very stretched tube. The next sixty kilometres should be relaxing.

The creeping potato vine is in bloom, jasmine hangs from stone walls and spiders parachute from webs attacking zee stoopid cyclist. East of Nantes, the Promenade Bellevue lives up to its name, with bench seats stationed every twenty metres for couples to sit and hold hands while watching the Loire roll past. A teenage girl throws her arms around a young man and they kiss. I look the other way and almost ride into a fence. Their giggles follow me down the path. My first bridge crossing is like riding through a cage, girders loom overhead. It mirrors the set of a World War Two movie. The Nazi tanks lumber slowly across as I pretend I'm the only French Resistance fighter wearing lycra. I reach into my back pocket for my trusty revolver and find a energy bar. The Director yells 'cut' and orders me to remove the helmet, once and for all.

The countryside opens up across the river, pastures of rape are in golden bloom; long rows of asparagus look ready for picking and the fruit trees are pink and white glory. But best of all, up ahead is a Supermache selling inner tubes that fit my bike. I buy two. And a repair kit. No need to worry. Who gets three punctures in three days? As I pack the tubes into my already overweight panniers, I gaze across the landscape. A supermarche on a hill surrounded by vineyards, a stone church steeple rising above a distant village and a farmer's ancient Renault station wagon lumbering along a side road. How very French.

Jacques and Claire are a French-Canadian couple, who have retired to Cannes. Perhaps it's the balmy weather of the south that convinced them to cycle along the Loire. We ride together for awhile, exchanging stories. They're shocked at how bad the weather is. I look up at the sky, a few patchy clouds, a light breeze, the sun valiantly trying to warm the day. 'It looks fine to me,' I say.

'We started on the west coast, further south,' says Jacques, 'It rained every day.'

'We caught the TGV here, hoping for an improvement,' adds Claire. She looks up, a cloud moves ominously above us. I notice they both have waterproof panniers. Mine are made of a thick coarse material, the type that repels rain for a few minutes, then gets incredibly heavy when drenched. Jacques and Claire are riding European sit-up style bikes, strong and dependable with wide tyres. They're slower than my hybrid, but can carry more and deal with the changes of road surface much easier. We bounce along an unpaved section of track, dodging puddles from last night's rain.

At Thouare-sur-Loire, they stop for lunch. Jacques shakes my hand as I depart. Claire says, 'Good luck with the punctures!' I look across to the cemetery on the far bank, flowers blooming among the gravestones. 'You mean good luck not getting punctures,' I reply.

I cross the bridge at Mauves-sur-Loire and ride among vineyards on gently sloping hills. Every thirty minutes, I stop to admire the rows of vines and check my front tyre. It could use more air. Up ahead is a pressed-metal mechanics workshop, outside the front door, a air-compressor with gauge. I poke my head into the workshop. No-one is around. I unwind the hose.

'Bonjour!' His voice is cheery, booming. He wears overalls and has curly hair and a big grin. The owner.

'Bonjour.' I reply, holding up the airhose. 'D'accord?' I ask.

'Oui, oui,' he says, 'Avez vous adapteur?'

I hold up my adaptor and begin screwing it onto the valve. He takes the nozzle from me and together we pump up both tyres. He begins a long monologue in french. I have no idea what he's saying and politely interrupt with 'Je suis desole, je ne parle pas francais.' He laughs and continues speaking in slower, but still incomprehensible, french. I nod and say 'oui' wherever possible. He gestures to ask where I'm heading. That's easy. 'Allemagne,' I say, confidently. Germany. I don't know the french word for Switzerland. And Basle is on the border with Germany and France. He whistles through crooked teeth.

When we're finished, he grabs my water bottle from it's cage and shakes it around. It's half-full. He points to my grimy hands and leads me inside, indicating the sink in the kitchen. While I wash my hands, he fills my bottle with a cold jug of water from the fridge. I notice his lunch is half-eaten on the table. A salad with saucisse. He's interrupted his lunch for me.

I'll repeat that.

A french workingman has interrupted his lunch to help somebody who can barely speak a word of his language. So much for cliches about the french being grumpy and unhelpful. In the three days I've been here, I've met nothing but kindness. On my two previous long visits to this country, it's been the same. I suspect the people who accuse the french of being surly and unfriendly are surly unfriendly tourists who trek no further than the sidewalk cafes of Paris. My friend comes to the door of his workshop to wave me goodbye. 'Bon voyage,' he calls. I cruise down a hill, clocking 50 kph, for the first time this trip, on properly-inflated tyres. I can't help but smile.

For lunch, I enter a bar and seven men look at me. The bartender says, 'Bonjour.' I reply, confidently, 'Bonjour manger.' Perhaps I should have put a comma in there somewhere, and a question mark. Whatever. Saying 'hello eat' is bound to get attention. The bartender points to the dining area in the next room. I sneak in and am greeted by an attractive young waitress who points me to the only vacant table. A half-empty (half-full) bottle of house red is conspicuous next to the knife and fork. To compensate for all the effort I put into changing a tyre this morning, I order an entree of mixed buffet, followed by steak and frites, with chocolate mousse for dessert. Formule Dejeuner. Cost? Euro10.50. That's about sixteen dollars, Australian or American. I can finish off the red if I wish.

The afternoon ride is splendid. The Loire to my right and vineyards to my left before I take a detour through le Fosse Nuef, an enchanting forest of swaying trees and amplified birdsong. A bubbling stream provides bass accompaniment to the birds. I seriously consider turning around and riding through again. And again.

In Ancenis, the locals have their priorities in order. A football field is afforded maximum Loire River frontage. The church and art museum are relegated to water glimpses. Workmen arrange cobblestones in a new section of the forecourt beside the river. The sun is now shining brightly. I sit on a garden seat and watch their artistry, but really I'm just waiting for the boulangerie to open for afternoon trade. A cafe eclair and sunshine.

I cycle along every street of Le-Mesnil-en-Vallee, which curiously seems to be on a hill, looking for the bed and breakfast accommodation. I finally spy a discrete sign above the doorbell. Madam welcomes me by waving for me to go around the back through the garden. Her Labrador eagerly graffitis my lycra with dirty paw prints. They need a wash anyway. My room is in the attic. Huge wooden beams criss-cross the ceiling at a height of 1.5 metres. Not even Napoleon could walk around here without stooping. It takes me only three minutes to bang my head. Merde! The owner,

Nadia is so apologetic she offers me numerous glasses of Pinot to ease the pain. Much better than aspirin.

In the evening, Nadia drives me to a restaurant in the next town for dinner. She will pick me up after visiting her sick father in hospital. My table has a view of the Loire and the bridge to the village of Ingrandes. I have three courses, again. Asparagus soup, fish stew (although the french description is much more elegant), and fruit salad with sorbet. As Nadia has plied me with too much vin, I order a beer. At the table next to mine, two women sit with their laptops open, facing each other. They quote figures over the screens, before typing. I wonder if they're playing computer battleships. Left 17? Miss. Right 5? Hit! The older woman consults her diary before entering more figures. The food arrives, and they suspend Battleship Francaise until après dessert.

It's nine o'clock in the evening and still light outside. The young lovers of this morning are replaced by an old couple, walking slowly on the path beside the Loire. They are holding hands.

Accommodation: Loire Chamilles B&B, 9 rue de l'Ecole, Le-Mesnil-en-Vallee. Friendly hosts, garden shed for the bike, good breakfast, unreliable wi-fi, charming room in the attic but watch your head! My score: 15/20 (if you don't bump your head) 12/20 (if you do).

Route tips: Ancenis is a picturesque town, worth checking out. You should ride the off-road path through le Fosse Neuf, a lovely section. Don't forget to pack a spare tube and tube repair kit! There are numerous vineyards and wineries on the south side of the Loire.

If you want to take your time, there are many wine makers who'll gladly ply you with samples of the vin!

Distance cycled today: 72km

Actual distance: 65km

What I should have said today: 'Madam, do you have a chainsaw? There are some hard wooden beams in my room I need to remove.'

Chapter Three

Le-Mesnil-en-Vallee to Angers

The Loire River does not glide gracefully along. It sucks and gurgles and coughs. I stand on the bank listening to a sound akin to an asthmatic in a cigar lounge. This cacophony is augmented by frogs and birds. French frogs don't croak, they make a cackling sound similar to an Australian wattle bird, halfway between a bird laughing and slowly being strangled. For the first three days I kept looking into the trees trying to spot the offending species. Perhaps the sound they make is fear... they are sometimes on the menu in these parts.

Today, the cycle path takes me across the Loire to La Basse Ille. As well as the pastures of grazing cattle and fields of rape, this island boasts the Lenin Cafe. Unfortunately closed when I arrive, it's an old stone building with a poster of Uncle Vladimir, his arm held high, his fist not clenched in revolution but holding a mobile phone. Perhaps he's trying to get reception on this far-away island? Karl Marx looks down fondly in the background. The Lenin Cafe hosts music nights and debates. I can't see a menu in the window, but I hope it's borscht, stroganov and potato dumplings washed down with vodka. Two hundred metres along the road is the Société Boule where old men meet in the evening to smoke and drink and toss heavy balls around. My son and I played boules a few years ago in Provence. We spent hours in a dirt car park perfecting our version of the peculiar backhand boule toss. It was immensely satisfying tossing such a heavy shiny perfectly round object, with the aim of crashing into your opponents boule to send it spinning away from the jack. Lawn bowls for the Chuck Norris generation.

At Challonnes-sur-Loire I buy a tartelette de fruit and sit in front of the Notre Dame. No, not that one. As I'm about to take the first bite, a motorcyclist dismounts and spits at his feet, making a hacking sound not unlike the Loire. I wait until he's well out of sight before crunching down on the perfect pastry. A young woman postie (post person?) cycles by on a velo electrique. I can't resist asking if I can snap a photo. It's a beautiful bike, flash yellow in colour with whitewall tyres. I'm tempted to suggest we swap. Her bike looks capable of carrying my load. Before I finish the pastry another woman cycles past. On her handlebars, flowers are growing in the front basket, window-box style. I wonder if she smells their scent with the wind?

I look at my bike, a Specialized Hybrid with twenty-one gears I transported from my house in the Blue Mountains, Australia. It's fire-engine red and has two simple panniers at the back. The handlebars are decorated with a Garmin to measure distance, altitude gain, speed and my heart rate, now pounding at a comfortable 82 beats per minute after cake, thank you. Next to the Garmin is a GoPro Video Camera, normally favoured by daredevils jumping off cliffs or skiers slaloming down near-vertical pistes. The camera is much safer with me, recording path after path through the forest. Before buying the camera, I reasoned with my wife that I could show her highlights of the trip. She grunted, a credible impression of Marge Simpson.

Back on the bike, I cycle slowly along the Loire bank until midday when a picturesque riverside village appears, as if on cue. My lunch today surpasses anything so far on this trip. The outdoor cafe is so close to the Loire, I could spit into the flow, if I was a French motorcyclist. In the courtyard square are ten tables in the sun. I select the only table in the shade. I order three courses... naturally. A simple seafood terrine followed by a rich beef bourguignon and finished with a ice-creamy custardy thingy. The waitress spends an inordinate amount of time helping me set up my wi-fi, so I can tell my wife what I've just consumed. More Marge impressions follow. On Skype, I show her vision of my dessert. She tells me the season is turning cold and bleak in the mountains.

I close the computer and sit back, order a beer and watch the Loire flow by. I gesture to the waitress that I'll leave if they need to use my table for more guests. In broken English, she assures me I can stay as long as I like. I order another drink. Again, the image of surly French waiters is drowned beside the fast-flowing Loire.

The meal? If you must know... Euro 11.50 in total. I'd pay that just for the vantage point of this chair beside the river!

Finally, I leave and ride slowly into Angers, on a dirt track beside a lake. Afternoon joggers compete for space with walkers and we cyclists, dodging puddles. At Lac de Maine, windsurfers pirouette across the surface of the water, their boards make a rhythmic slapping sound.

I round a bend, cross a little bridge and cruise onto the promenade along the Maine River, a tributary of the Loire. Office buildings on the far bank gleam in the afternoon sun. I have arrived in Angers. To celebrate, I get a flat tyre. Three punctures in three days! This can't go on.

Within seconds of finishing the repair, a woman on a bike offers assistance. I ask directions to a bike shop. She tries to explain, but it's too complicated. Another woman stops to help. 'Simple, premiere a gauche, deuxieme a droite, droites centain metres...' When she sees I can't understand the convoluted directions, she offers to take me as it's her local bike shop.

We walk together and tell our stories using mime and elementary words. She's lived in Angers her whole life, travelled extensively, but loves the city. Walks every day. Saves stupid Australian cyclists once a week?

The bike shop owner quickly finishes his current job and begins fitting a new tyre and tube for me. I love the French words for bike tube - chambre de air. I buy an extra tyre as a spare. The price is eye-poppingly cheap. I bow profusely in thanks. The ride into Angers - oh look there's a cathedral, there's a chateau, there's a fountain - is like starting the journey anew. The ancient buildings are wonderful, but not as pleasing as my new tyre!

Angers crackles with energy on this sparkling day. University students sit beside the river, punching commands into iPads and laptops. Young people, helmetless of course, cycle across the park. The sidewalk cafes are crowded, an old woman leads her small chien to a vacant chair and sits down, a waiter appearing immediately. The dog licks the shoe of the woman. I stand at a bus shelter, studying the town map, looking for an outlying village named le Plessis-Grammoire. It's too outlying to be on the map, so I remount and head north-east, vaguely. The city has bike lanes, sometimes shared with the commuter bus, so I pedal faster than usual to keep ahead of the 318 all stops to... somewhere. The driver gives me space.

Eventually, after a few wrong turns, I see a sign for my village and breathe a sigh of relief. The idea of phoning my B&B and asking for directions in French is unappealing. To celebrate being on the correct road, I stop at a fruit barn and buy two blood oranges and three hundred grams of sugared peanuts. One tart, one sweet.

At the Bed and Breakfast, I have the house to myself. I prepare dinner in the kitchen, scrambled eggs with jambon and a pain complet. I miss the three course meal already, but the huge dining room makes up for it. I lounge on the regal high-backed chairs, prowl the expanse of carpet to the fireplace, rest my elbow against the mantel and declaim bad poetry to the emptiness of the room.

Accommodation: Angers-Charmance B&B, 25 rue des Quatre-Vents, Andard. (actually much closer to le Plessis-Grammoire, than Andard!). Comfortable room upstairs, large dining/lounge area for guests, wi-fi only available outside the main house, hearty breakfast, space for bike in foyer or garage. Check-in after 5pm. My score: 15/20.

Route tips: A combination of quiet back roads and paths beside the river makes for an easy day cycling. The road on La Basse Ille is lovely in spring, with flowers and crops and little traffic to disturb your appreciation of the landscape. Anyone for boules? Once you're back on the south side of the Loire... how many wineries do you want to visit? The choice is endless. The detour to Angers is recommended and I'd suggest finding accommodation in town if you feel like a restaurant dinner at night as there are no alternatives near the B&B. If you want to self-cater, the B&B is a perfect option.

Distance cycled today: 65km

Actual Distance: 52km

What I should have said: 'I hate you ******* useless chambre de air! Hate! Hate! Hate!'

Chapter Four

Angers to Savigny-en-Veron

Breakfast this morning is an extravagance. A fresh baguette, home-made confiture, pate de foie, quiche Lorraine, stewed apricots and yoghurt. And... chocolate mousse. For breakfast! All washed down with a jug of coffee.

The first few kilometres are ridden at breakneck speed, a combination of downhill and caffeine. On the Loire side of the road are long lines of butter lettuce, waiting to be harvested, on the other are alternate rows of lonceria pile moss green, potcatilla goldfinger and hydrangea phantoms. Yep, I read the stickers on the stakes at the start of each row.

I detour into the hills to visit Coutures, the village where perhaps France's most interesting peasant woman lived. Madame Ernestine Chassebeouf was born in 1910 and lived her entire life in this region, taking care of her husband, a garden and the chickens. A simple country existence for a woman with an enquiring mind and a forceful personality. Late in life, Madame began writing punchy letters lobbying politicians, townspeople and the editors of newspapers on a variety of issues, particularly the debate over the role of free lending libraries in France. Her naive and unique writing style impressed two prominent French journalists who arranged publication of her missives, in three volumes, titled (in translation) **Ernestine writes everywhere**. The collections were only published in French, so alas, I have not read the originals. But I picture

Madame Ernestine as an 'every-Mother' - wise, witty and truculent. When she spoke, people listened. The French, so beloved of their rural heritage, even though most people live in cities, and so enamoured of the old-fashioned habit of penning letters in a formal style, would have loved Madame's homilies. Her story glows in celebration of a life lived in the moment and for the community.

For such a small village, Coutures packs a punch. Troglodyte dwellings built into the chalky cliffs are now used by locals as caves for wine or garden sheds; a walking trail leads visitors to ancient lavoirs; and the Chateau de Montsabert stands regal on the opposite hill. Cycling out of the village, after paying my respects to the literary memory of Madame Chassebeouf, I see an old moulin on a hill. Wooden and curiously animate, I expect it to start spinning at the next gust. A blackbird flies between the arms, as if to prove me wrong.

Back on the Loire, from a distance the village of Le Thourel seems to float on the river. It only has one street, a few stone houses rising above the levee and jasmine dangling invitingly over each garden gate.

For the next thirty kilometres it's Troglodyte-central with cafes, wineries and art galleries burrowing into the cliff-face... and the tourist wallets. I stop at one gallery, nod at the elegantly dressed woman behind the counter and wander the cool interior. The prices insult my bicycle sensibility. You want how much for... that? A busload of tourists pull up outside and the woman moves from behind the counter to greet them. I slink away, relieved.

Ahead on the road is a man riding a recumbent cycle, a flag dancing gaily from the pole above the reclining seat. I cycle alongside and introduce myself. Joseph is retired after years in the French military. 'Engineer,' he says, 'not fighting, no battle for me.' He grins and I like him immediately. He tells me he has a bad back and the recumbent is a recent purchase to overcome 'sitting in my house, wondering.' He pedals easily at a medium pace, but whenever we slow for an intersection, the wobbles begin. I comment on this and Joseph shrugs, 'I am... enfant on this velo.' His eyes twinkle, 'But soon...' He pedals faster and zips away before slowing once again to wait for me. Like middle-aged men everywhere, talk turns to our sons. His has travelled widely, been to Australia, and is now living in Hong Kong. Joseph talks of visiting him soon, a wistful look on his face. I tell him my youngest son is named Joseph. We laugh.

I suggest lunch in the next town. Joseph shakes his head, 'No, Merci. I have eaten already, but I will join you. For Perrier.' It is past lunch by the time we arrive in Saumur and the restaurant can only offer steak and frites. 'Le menu, ferme,' explains the waitress. Steak and frites and a basket of bread, washed down with pichet de rosé. I can hardly complain. Joseph makes do with mineral water. He tells me of an organization he has joined, called 'warm showers' - a group of cyclists and travellers who offer a sofa, or bed, and a shower for fellow travellers, for free. Like everyone I have met so far, Joseph is on a budget. He nods at my extravagant lunch and says, 'I 'ad baguette and fromage.' I mop my sauce with the last of the bread.

In the afternoon, we cycle together and cure the world of all it's sins and maladies. If only someone would listen. Joseph sighs and talks about his next trip, to Hong Kong. He admires my freedom, wonders how I can do all this travelling for months on end. 'I am a writer,' I explain. 'Many books?' he asks. 'Vingt,' I say, holding up one hand, four times, just in case he thinks I'm asking for wine instead of saying twenty. He whistles. 'Many books,' he repeats. 'Never enough,' I add. At Montsoreau, where the Loire and la Vienne River meet, we shake hands and exchange email addresses. Joseph wants me to send a video of him riding the recumbent. I promise I will.

I've stayed at the Bed and Breakfast at Savigny-en-Veron before. The owners are kindly folk who provide large self-contained rooms on the top-floor of their stately house. I love Madam's breakfast - seven home-made jams.

In the evening, I cycle to dinner in Avione on a track that leads me through fields of wheat. It's weird cycling at 7.30 at night, knowing the light will hold for another two hours. At the one restaurant in town, I indulge again. Three triangles of superb pear and goats cheese pastry for entree, chicken in a pot with a side of vegetables for main. Even the swedes taste delicious! In deference to the creaking of my bicycle, I refrain from dessert. Only for tonight. Cycling home, I pass on old man on his ancient velo. He's weaving from side to side... could be the bike, or the bar-tabac where he's spent the evening. He hums a drunken tune to the evening. I wish I knew the words to join in.

Accommodation: Chevire B&B, 11 rue Basse, Savigny en Veron, Indre et Loire. Comfortable rooms, huge breakfasts (I rank blackberry confiture premier class!), friendly hosts. A large downstairs area for guests and also outdoor seating for coffee if the weather agrees. An acceptably low tariff! Price E43-50 My score: 16/20.

Route tips: You are now in troglodyte territory. Perhaps plan a detour to Coutures, or the area near Doue-la-Fontaine where there are a number of villages ancient. Doue is also the 'rose capital of France' and has a number of wineries surrounding the town. Or, if you're feeling less adventurous, stick to the Loire pathway and enjoy the flat pedalling and tourist stops. There's a village every few kilometres to refuel… in all sorts of ways.

Distance cycled today: 90km

Actual distance: 75km

What I should have said: 'Dear Joseph, allow me to buy you lunch, s'il vous plait?

Chapter Five

Savigny en Veron to Rochecorbon

The day begins with the application of a turbo hairdryer to my cycling knicks. No, I'm not wearing them at the time. With limited clothes, I have to be inventive. The tailwind I've enjoyed since the Atlantic Ocean has been replaced by its unpleasant cousin, the headwind, which I'll call 'Nigel the tetevent.' Nigel complains that in French he should be known as face de vent. Nigel is a real bully too, blustery and cold, sweeping off the Loire. The road on the levee provides no shelter. Even the clacking of the frogs seems muted by Nigel's cold breath.

In relief, I turn off to look at the 15th Century Chateau D'Usse on the Indre River. Reportedly the inspiration for Sleeping Beauty, it's a wedding-cake concoction of stone with whimsical turrets that perhaps takes advantage of the fairytale connection a little too much. I prefer the Renaissance Chapel built on the slope leading up to the Chateau, framed by an oak forest. I admire an estate that has its own church. Imagine the master of the manor declaring, 'Excusez-moi, Dear, I'm off to commune with God before dinner.'

Nigel doesn't believe in God, just his own domain. My helmet is pushed back on my head, at a how-do-you-do angle. Nigel's laugh is sinister. The path leads away from the Loire into a secluded forest of dappled light and birdsong, with pheasants in the undergrowth. As soon as I enter these rarefied environments, I take a deep breath, as if all that greenery will suck the available oxygen from the atmosphere. This forest lives and breathes. My bike rattles over hard packed gravel. At a crossroads, I lean the bike against a tree and walk under the canopy of green. The ground is soft and spongy. I sit on a dead log and take a long swig of water. Not a sound penetrates here but the bird song. In Australia, in the bush near my house, where there are canyon walls close by, I'd yell 'coooeee' and wait to hear an echo. I call once here, the sound soaks into the trees and undergrowth. Silence.

At Brehement, I return to the levee. Nigel cracks his knuckles and begins blowing again. I stop at a boulangerie and order a Paris Brest, named in honour of the bike race. In the shape of a bicycle wheel, it consists of choux pastry with a praline cream, sprinkled with almonds. So much decadence for so little money. The owner brings me a glass of water and happily fills my bottle. Two cyclists walk into the bakery and rub their hands in chill. Nigel has been picking on them as well. 'Vent Froid' I say. The older man answers. I think it's a swear word in French. They're cycling to Fountainbleu, a week away. I tell them my destination. The man smiles and says, 'bon courage.' It's a thought as sweet as a Paris Brest.

At Savonnieres, a pretty town on the River Cher, I have lunch in the only open cafe. The waitress has jet black hair firmly swept back in a tight ponytail. She wears high heels and is haughty beyond belief. She's not rude, it's just the way she carries herself. Her nose is long and it points more to the ceiling than the floor. I peruse the menu, recognising only a few dishes. She stands over me. I tentatively point at my selection.

She shakes her head, 'Non. You will not like that.'

I suspect it's blood sausage.

Madame makes a pained face. She waits. I'm too intimidated to argue.

'Confit de Canard,' I suggest.

Madame agrees.

It's hard to believe that something as delicious as Confit de Canard comes out of a tin. All that fat, with a crispy skin. It's my default dish in France, particularly when accompanied by potatoes cooked in duck fat. Today's serving arrives with frites and salad. I ask for another carafe of water, hoping Madame will understand I'm cycling, so alcohol is unwise. She shrugs and brings another bottle of tap water. When I'm finished, two middle-aged women walk in and order champagne, chevre fromage and duck. I love the French. No salad and mineral water here, just duck and goats cheese. Fatty food, thin women.

And so to Tours, my fourth visit to the regal town in twenty years. On my first, I stayed in a tiny room above a desolate cafe alongside the Loire. From memory, it cost the equivalent of five dollars. I pretended I was a poet in a garret, looking out from a battered dormer window at the fast-flowing river, waiting for inspiration... or tuberculosis. I spoke no French and the taciturn man behind the counter counted off the francs I offered in the palm of my timid hand. The cafe seemed the exclusive domain of old men in berets. It smelt of damp carpet, cigarette smoke and alcohol. A rusting bicycle stood watch at the doorway. I remember banging my head every time I walked to the toilet upstairs. I didn't write any poetry during my stay.

On this sunny Saturday, everyone is sitting outdoors at cafes. In the old quarter, the square is crowded with restaurant tables, waiters pushed to the edge of frantic. Empty bottles of wine are removed and replaced in the blink of an eye. Cigarette smoke hangs like an question-mark. Everyone is wearing light-coloured clothing, as if to wear black on such a day would be to shun the weather gods. In the very centre of the square, on the cobblestones, a monocyclist wows the crowd with balancing tricks. The carry-case for his cycle is littered with coins. I bet he never gets a flat tyre.

Nigel has gone off in a sulk. I pedal along wide bike paths in parks where the local residents, are they called TOURists, picnic on blankets or walk their dogs. I watch a game of football on a field of dirt beside the Loire before settling myself in the booth of a cafe, the only person indoors. I've had enough of the sun. The owner helps me get a wi-fi connection. Computers... merde!

In the late afternoon, après cafe ice-cream s'il vous plait, I cycle along the Loire to Rochecorbon, a rich suburb of Tours. My Bed and Breakfast is a suburban maison on top of a very steep hill. The owner greets me briskly and suggests I leave the bike under the house. She shows me my room, large with an adjoining room for les enfant, where I park my panniers. I suggest an early breakfast time. She raises an eyebrow, shaking her head and uttering one word to deny my request, 'Dimanche!' We agree on 8am.

For dinner, I cruise down to the centre of the village, still wearing my lycra. It's the first time I've eaten in my 'day suit.' I feel foolish walking into the restaurant. Couples, dressed in elegant casual, study the wine list rather than look at my black leg-warmers. C'est gauche!

I hide my embarrassment by ordering four courses. To paraphrase my wife, cycling is just an interlude between meals. A plate of jambon Espagna followed by poisson swimming in a butter sauce fills the hole. The cheese plate and a delicious apple tart with cinnamon ice-cream builds a mound where my flat stomach once lived. Luckily, lycra stretches. I pretend that cycling back up the hill to my Bed and Breakfast will burn off all the calories from dinner. It would... if I cycled it until Christmas.

Accommodation: La Haute Gatinieres, Chemin de bois Soleil, Rochecorbon. Comfortable rooms, professional hosts, good breakfast, slow wi-fi. Located atop a mighty big hill means a good view, but could be difficult to find without a map and/or a GPS. Price: E58. My score: 15/20.

Route tips: How many Chateaus do you want to visit? You are spoiled for choice in this region. I'd suggest a detour to Chinon, a charming village on the river Cher. If you have children, read them the Sleeping Beauty story and then arrange a visit to Chateau d'Usse. Spend at least an afternoon in Tours, wandering the old town. Perhaps stay the night. I'd recommend the Hotel Colbert, rue de Colbert, Tours. Friendly hosts, ask for a room overlooking the garden. Price: E45-61. My score (from four years ago): 16/20.

Distance cycled today: 72km

Actual distance: 68km

What I should have said: 'Bonsoir Monsieur-dame, but of course, lycra is considered formal evening wear in Australia!'

Chapter Six

Rochecorbon to Chaumont-sur-Loire

Sunday morning. The French are sensible late-risers. I cycle the quiet back roads to Vouvray, a renown wine region on the Loire. But, not this early on a weekend. The vintners are asleep, dreaming of the perfect harvest. There's nothing for me to do but cycle slowly and daydream, enjoying the warming sun.

At Montlouis-sur-Loire, I hook up with Jill and Brin, two retirees from Canada. Jill is a bubbly nurse, Brin a quiet, self-effacing doctor. I joke that I'll feel better if I have an accident with them around. Brin says he was a specialist obstetrician and he'll be happy to help should I fall pregnant, rather than fall off my bike. I ask about their motivations for cycling.

'Easy to explain, really,' says Jill, glancing toward Brin, 'we spent our life around patients, people incapacitated, in one way or another.' She pedals a little bit faster as we crest a hill, 'You never know how long you've got,' she says, 'better to make use of good health.'

I smile at such simple wisdom. I like this couple very much. Brin looks around at the vineyards either side of the bike path, before adding, 'Perhaps this is the best antidote to old age.' He motions for me to move over to the right of the path to let a lycra-clad cyclist on a racing bike cycle past. The young man nods and sits up in the saddle before powering away. Brin and I look at each other.

'I didn't hear him,' I say.

Brin touches the tiny mirror extending from his helmet. 'Always good to know what's behind, to see where you've been.' he says, 'It's why I take photos. I've got hundreds from this trip already.'

'And what do you do, Jill?' I ask.

'I stand in Brin's photos!' she says. 'Me with chateau, me beside river, me in garden. I tell him to just take the photo without me.'

'It gives the picture a human scale, Jill.' Brin explains.

It's a long downhill ride into Amboise. Jill leads, Brin follows. I take the rear and spend a lonely few minutes missing my wife. She's not a cyclist.

At Amboise, a market is in full bloom. Jill and Brin are visiting the Chateau. I want lunch. We part, after the obligatory photo from Brin. Jill and me in front of the Chateau. We wish each other good health.

The Amboise market is alongside the Loire, crowds park a kilometre away and walk along the levee to do their shopping. Families wander the dirt-covered area, sampling the food on offer. I'm surprised by the number of children here, shopping with their parents. They look to be enjoying themselves.

The French market is a glorious institution that challenges the domination of corporations and soulless supermarkets.

On sale today are every type of fruit and vegetable in season, glowing in ripe splendour. One fromage stall has over sixty different cheeses on display, many local. The smell entices me to linger and watch. Two women behind the counter greet each customer. No-one buys just one cheese. Next door is a saucisse maker. He beckons me near and offers a slice of chewy meat.

'Porc,' he says.

'Tres bon,' I reply.

Encouraged, he cuts me a slice from another saucisse, and another, and another. I taste each one.

'Canard.'

'Agneau.'

'Cheval.'

'Chevre.'

Finally, he hands me a slice without commenting on what it is. I hesitate. He smiles,

'Bambi.'

I chomp down on the spicy saucisse. He approves. I buy a saucisse de porc for a few euros, wondering how I'm going to eat it all. A few stalls away is a counter buckling under the weight of bread. The depth of colour in each loaf is proof enough of their quality. For a single Euro, I buy a crisp doorstop of a loaf. Next door I purchase a tomato. Lunch is ready. I wander the market. Cages of ducks and chickens are stacked five high next to cages of cats. Pets and poultry? A seafood stall has a long line of customers, mostly old ladies with shopping trolleys, their eyes keenly seeking out the freshest wares. I always love the way old ladies pay for their shopping. They open their purse and slowly hand over coin after coin, rarely wanting to pay with a note. The stallholder waits patiently. The last coin is handed over. Without fail, the stallholder wishes the customer a 'bonne journee.'

I take my lunch and ride through the cobblestone lanes of the old town. Beside a stream, on a patch of green grass, I lay out my wares for a picnic. With my Swiss army knife, I slice saucisse and tomato. The crust of the bread has cracks that remind me of an old stone wall, solid, long-lasting, dependable. Pain complet, indeed. The saucisse is salt and fat and garlic and meat and everything I was hoping for.

As I'm eating, two ducks waddle close. I toss them a few crumbs from my bread. They catch them in eager beaks. One duck leans close to my tomato. She doesn't like the smell and satisfies herself with more crumbs. I don't offer the saucisse. No matter how much I eat, I cannot hope to finish this feast. The ducks fly off in search of more appealing dishes. I slowly rise, both knees creaking with the effort. I have spent too long here in the sun. I cruise back into town. The market is closing down. I walk along the levee where there are lovers seats in the garden. Shaped in the figure eight, the seat enables couples to face each other and kiss, both with one eye on the romantic Loire. I wish Brin and Jill were here, for a photo on this seat.

Sunday afternoon rolls along like the Loire, slow and languid. I barely raise a sweat as I cycle past vineyards and villages. I arrive early at the Bed and Breakfast on the river in Chaumont-sur-Loire. The owner had emailed me directions, 'We are between the Loire and the Chateau.'

And, indeed, the Chateau towers above the main street of Chaumont. Whilst leading me to my room, the owner, Jacky tells me of the famous people who have lodged at the Chateau. Nostradamus. Catherine de Medici. Benjamin Franklin. I nod, impressed. I'm even more impressed with the view from my front window, an expansive panorama of the Loire. A few old wooden sailing boats are moored at the jetty. I quickly change out of lycra and walk into town. At the Office de Tourisme, I ask the lady where I might find a beer?

She says, 'You are after fabrique artisanale?'

I look dumbfounded. 'Ahh, no, a biere, s'il vous plait.'

She directs me to a cafe two hundred metres away. 'They sell biere, fabrique artisanale,' she states.

The cafe is very small, two tables indoors, two outdoors. I take a seat outside to watch the Loire. The owner brings me a bottle of beer and a glass. I read the label. It is from the micro-brewery, two doors down the street. The penny drops.

And so does the beer, in long gulps. It's very refreshing. I order another and glory in the French who produce so much food and alcohol locally that a person like me can happily travel the country eating regionally and never be disappointed. I raise a silent toast to a civilised culture and drink my fabrique artisanale.

I am the only resident tonight in the Bed and Breakfast. The owners, not unexpectedly, recommend the restaurant next door, run by their son. It's an appealing old eating house, with yellow stucco walls, an open fireplace, curtains like hessian bags decorated with flowers draped over the curtain rods, rust-red tiles on the floor and a matching yellow tablecloth. I dine on white asparagus, rabbit with mustard sauce and a dessert of cassis and framboise sorbet, washed down with a pichet de rosé. All done by nine o'clock in the evening, I wander into the village.

The swallows circle the chateau and swoop low over the river. A dog barks from the opposite bank. A young couple putter by on a scooter, the girl driving, her boyfriend wraps one arm around her waist and holds the rear of the seat with the other. Neither are wearing helmets. I sit on a bench seat on the levee and watch the dusk settle on the river.

Accommodation: La maison de percheur, Chaumont-sur-Loire (at the foot of the Chateau). Comfortable bed, lovely location with a view of the river, friendly hosts, sitting room for guests, good restaurant nearby. Price: E65-70. My score: 16/20.

Route tips: Certainly visit Amboise, but also consider a side trip to the Chateau de Chenonceau for its immaculate gardens and lovely location on, and I mean on, the river Cher. Of all the Loire Chateaus, I'd choose Chenonceau. A bike path detours from the Loire through the Forest d'Amboise to Chenonceau (approx 20 kilometres) before winding back through vineyards and open fields to Chaumont-sur-Loire (another 26 kilometres).

Distance cycled today: 50km

Actual distance: 36km

What I should have said: 'Oui, Madame, ja'i envie d'une fabrique artisanale.'

Chapter Seven

Chaumont-sur-Loire to Orleans

From my window, I watch the morning mist shimmer over the surface of the Loire. A big breakfast and an extra layer of clothes are in order. It's clear and cold, a finger-numbing six degrees as I begin to pedal slowly along the river road.

Despite the bright sunshine, I'll blame the wind chill for what happens next. A few kilometres past Cande-sur-Bevron, lost in thought over whether to choose a cafe éclair or Paris-Brest pastry at the next boulangerie, I miss the sign for the Eurovelo 6. Or, in my defence, I follow another sign that I think substitutes for the Eurovelo. Merde!

Somehow, I end up in the Foret Domaniale de Russy, which, according to my map, is large and bisected by two D roads. Pity I can't find either. I ride slowly along the forest path, listening to the ever-present birdsong. Dirt tracks lead off north and south every few hundred metres. I assume I'm heading east. I hope I'm heading east. Spider webs stretch across the forest track, like gossamer finishing tape at the 100 metre sprint. My medal? A face full of cobwebs. Today is my first one-hundred-kilometre section. I imagine it'll be one-hundred-ten kilometres, if I can find my way out.

The Foret Domaniale de Russy has an amazing network of tracks. I ride them all for an hour. But wait, is that a jogger or a track-suited mass murderer running towards me? He appears as surprised to see me as I am to encounter him on this lonely bush track.

'Ou est Blois?' I ask.

'Perdue?' he suggests, perhaps unnecessarily, but who am I to criticise.

'Oui,' I say.

He turns and points from where he's come, 'Gauche, tout droit. Blois,' he says, simply. He reinstalls his earplugs and waves me au revoir. Left, straight ahead, Blois. Could it be any easier? Well, yes, actually. Because as I reach the suggested left turn, I notice there are two tracks heading in that direction. I choose the widest path and five minutes later, I'm on the D765 being buffeted by trucks and tractors heading into Blois. I am very pleased to see the Loire once more.

Blois is a handsome town on a hill overlooking the river. This area of such bucolic charm has a bloodstained past. Blois was the location of the first ritual murder in France, nine hundred years ago. The victims were Jews who became known as the martyrs of Blois. They were allegedly massacred because one of their number was falsely accused by a peasant of murdering a child. In 12th century Justice, the accuser was subjected to the 'water test'. The peasant was ordered to step into a large deep pool of water. He did not drown, but floated. This was treated as proof he was telling the truth. Therefore, the accused Jew must be guilty. It is believed up to thirty Jewish citizens were massacred because one peasant could float.

Blois is also the town from where Joan of Arc set out to liberate Orleans. I am now truly in Joan country, with her statue prominent in many villages. After a cafe éclair and one more check of the map, I follow the path east. For the first time, I witness water sports on the river. A kayaker slowly windmills close to the near bank while a speedboat pulls a wet-suited water skier along in ever-widening circles. The kayaker ignores the water skier, determinedly gazing across the fields as he makes slow, graceful progress.

Beaugency, where Joan of Arc lead a successful battle to capture the strategic bridge, is a fine town of ancient buildings and loitering teenagers. It's lunchtime and the students gather in laughing groups, enjoying the sunshine. One pony-tailed student juggles a football, the girls giggle as he traps it between his knees, a bow-legged jester. I cycle into the centre of town, where an elegant restaurant is open. Shiny tiled floor, wide balcony with cushioned chairs, well-dressed waiters… it's this, or more cycling.

Businessman in suits, finishing their coffee, look up as I tentatively enter. Could I be a courier in lycra? Non. The waitress offers me a table either indoors or outside? I suck it in and plonk myself down next to the two portly gentleman. The long booth seat is covered in rich brown leather. I put my backpack on the floor under the table and order the plat du jour. As usual, a large basket of bread and a carafe of water arrives soon after. I've half-emptied the basket before my tender, barely cooked steak arrives. It's fantastic. I mop up the juices with the last of the bread. The vegetables are delicious, even the zucchinis. The waitress refills my basket. I mop some more. I am the last to leave. It's thirty kilometres to Orleans and another ten to my lodgings in Checy.

After Meung-sur-Loire, I take a detour to Clery St Andre to look at the 15th century Basilica. It's a Gothic beauty, with glorious stained-glass windows and vaulted ceilings. The church houses the tombs of Louis XI and his wife. More importantly, it's also the resting place of Jean, the Count of Dunois also known as The Bastard of Orleans and Joan of Arc's companion. If I could choose one name this would be it. Imagine introducing yourself at parties, 'I am Jean, Count of Dunois, The Bastard of Orleans.' I ride away, mimicking a fencing duel, whispering to myself, 'Attendez moi, The Bastard of Orleans.' With one elaborate lunge, I almost ride into a ditch. A dog barks, in applause.

Which leads me to Orleans in the late afternoon. What a fine town it is. I nod in deference to Saint Joan, her statue prominent in the square, before wandering the vaulted interior of the Cathedral. I sit in the rear pew, trying to imagine a nineteen-year-old peasant girl leading an army. And for her valour? Soon after, she was burned at the stake. An old woman in a shawl, walks down the aisle and crosses herself in front of the altar. The last rays of the afternoon sun stream through the coloured glass windows. A dove coos from high above.

Time for a beer. And what better place to choose than Place du Matroi, with the enormous bronze statue by sculptor Denis Foyatier, of Joan of Arc on a horse, her sword drawn. I raise a Kronenbourg to our heroine and watch the afternoon town go about it's business. I play my favourite French outdoor cafe game - asking myself irrelevant questions.

Why do I dislike children who wear sunglasses?

Is brown an appropriate colour for a full-length overcoat worn by that gentleman admiring the statue?

Why does every second teenage girl wear ballet shoes?

Should we enact laws to prevent young men from wearing white trousers?

How did my glass empty so quickly?

Why is that waiter ignoring me?

The cycle to Checy is, understandably, slow and wandering. I follow the river which eventually leads me to the side door of the Bed and Breakfast. My room is small, overlooking a leafy garden. There are no restaurants in town. After one hundred and ten kilometres, I cannot manage the cycle back to Orleans. I dine in the Kebab shop. The owner is Tunisian. He speaks garbled English. I speak twisted mime. We entertain each other for the duration of my meal.

Accommodation: Les Courtils, rue de l'Ave, Checy. Ideal location on the Eurovelo path. Small room, however there is a large guest area to compensate. Wi-fi downstairs, a peaceful back deck and garden for guests. Bicycles can be stored safely on the back deck. Price: E52-60. My score: 15/20.

Route tip: Follow the signs! Do not get lost in the forest! Perhaps detour to the Chateau de Chambord, an imposing pile of French Renaissance architecture, the largest Chateau in the Loire Valley. A bicycle path leads you directly to the Chateau and its extensive parkland. Ideally, if you have time, spend two days exploring the region. Orleans has numerous accommodation options. There are limited eating places in Checy, so if you want a meal, it's back to Orleans.

Distance cycled today: 110km

Actual distance: 92km

What I should have said: 'I am The Bastard of Orleans, and I demand another steak, s'il vous plait?'

Chapter Eight

Orleans to Saint-Firmin-sur-Loire

I have decided to give my bicycle a name. After 500 kilometres on the Loire, he/she deserves a title.

Craig.

It's hardly inspiring, but allow me to explain. While this book is about my travels on the Loire, it sometimes seems to be more a catalogue of my eating habits. Excusez-moi. If it wasn't for Craig, I'd be hugely obese. This 21-speed bicycle is better than any weight-loss program yet devised. So, it had to be Jenny Craig, didn't it? And I'm baulking at riding Jenny across France. I feel no such scruples about Craig. He's a good bloke who can take a few knocks, like the time I left him outside the Rochecorbon Office de Tourisme without checking his balance and the wind, Nigel, no doubt, pushed him over. What a clatter, and he has the scars to prove it.

Today, Craig and I visit the 16th Century church at Germingy-des-Pres. It's a lovely simple building with a timber ceiling, long bench seats, chandelier lights and a basic font. Near the nave, pictures of the village soldiers from World War One have pride of place. On the back wall is a list of all the Priests, starting with Jehan Delacroix in 1589 and mysteriously finishing in 1984 with Albert Lenoir. I assume a Priest from outside the commune now does the honours. Very sad. What must Monsieur Lenoir have thought when he closed the door for the last time. A long line of Priests, stretching back to the Middle Ages, followed poor Albert down the street to the tabac, where no doubt, they all had one glass too many, before the ghosts wandered the village, listening to the dogs howl and the weather vane spin, waiting for the Church to appoint a new Priest.

I'm cheered at St-Benoit-sur-Loire by the lady in the boulangarie who sells me, for the princely sum of Euro 1.50, a Grande Mere. I've never known a Grandmother as sweet as this. It resembles a wedge of bread and butter pudding, with added custard and a subtle alcohol flavouring. Craig groans under the extra weight, but he only has to take me around the corner to the Abbey at St Benoit - another vaulted ceiling, leadlight-windowed, stone masterpiece. Inside, an old man talks authoritatively to a group of teenagers. And they listen! So do I. I like his voice. And a certain weighty Grandmother is telling me to rest, for a while.

St-Benoit-sur-Loire is a wonderful example of a French village, still very much alive, even with a dwindling population. From the town square, I can see a Pharmacy, a Charcuterie, an electronics shop, the Cafe de la Ville with tables outside, a Credit Agricole and my beloved boulangarie. Parked in the square is a van selling seafood. I imagine the fishmonger is there once or twice a week in the morning. Old ladies wheel their shopping trolleys around the square, everything they need is a stroll away. But, much more importantly, they meet in the square and chat. I imagine, over a Grande Mere.

The most prominent building on the square is, of course, the Mairie, centre of all the administrative aspects of the village. Around the corner is a small grocery store and another boulangerie. Can you imagine any town in Australia, or the USA, with a comparable population of only two thousand citizens, offering so much variety and... originality? I love the French resistance to strip shopping; to generic bakers and butchers; to having their administrative affairs mindlessly centralised. Long may they reign.

Craig's getting bored with this monologue, so we sluggishly roll away towards St-Florent. For the past few hours, storm clouds have been gathering. Craig tried to warn me, but I was too busy stuffing my face. When the downpour hits, I'm kilometres from any village, or adequate shelter. I huddle beside a hedgerow until the first front passes. A drip from the branch above drums on my helmet. I decide to make a dash for it. As soon as I'm in the saddle, the hailstones arrive. They're not big, but combined with the rain, I'm quickly soaked. Please let the next town have a bistro.

I squelch into a Chambre d'Hotel that appears to be empty, even though the tables are set for a meal service. Madame walks out from the kitchen. Her thick grey hair is tied up in a bun making her look more severe, more imposing as she appears from the shadows. She is wearing an apron, in her hand a wooden spoon. She looks at the puddle I'm standing in.

'Je suis desole, Madam, avez vous dejeneur?' I plead.

Maybe I even whimper, just a little. She begrudgingly nods her head and offers me a table in the corner. As she gets the menu, I take off my jacket and shoes and socks. I'm chilled to the bone. Outside the sun has returned and is shining on Craig. After ordering the Formule Menu, I take my shoes and socks out to the bike and drape them over the handlebars.

There's a cold wind blowing, not a hope of drying anything. Madame brings the first course, a pate de campagne and bread. While I'm eating this, she goes outside and sees my bike and patched up clothes-line. She exclaims loudly, the sound of someone whose restaurant entry has been converted to a laundry. I eat the last of the pate, expecting to be evicted forthwith.

Madame returns with some kindling, tut-tutting. She builds a roaring fire and arranges some chairs close to the hearth, gesturing that I should hang my clothes over them. I bow and say 'merci beaucoup' over and over. While waiting for my second course, confit de canard, I stand in front of the fireplace, Lord of the Manor. It's a late lunch, but there are no other diners. The duck is delicious. In this warm room, with this generous woman, burnt toast would have been wonderful. Madame and I have barely spoken. I wish I knew the French words for, 'You are my hero.' She brings in another log and nonchalantly tosses it on the fire, reels off rapid-fire French that I assume is about the wretched weather. Or perhaps about the smell coming from my still damp clothes? Either way, I nod agreement.

The meal finishes with fresh strawberries. I reluctantly shrug into the clothes, now dry and put my shoes back on. I'm warmed to the core by the meal and Madame's hospitality. A tip is in order. Outside the wind is still blowing and threatening to bring more storms. As I hop back on Craig, I see Madame clearing the dishes from my table. I wave. She nods in response.

Five kilometres from my accommodation for the evening, the rain returns. I exhaust my vocabulary of invective. The sky refuses to listen. Water trickles down my neck, drips from my helmet, squelches my shoes. On the banks of the Loire, the ducks stand unmoved by the downpour. The sound of car tyres on wet tarmac serenades the afternoon. I have transcribed in my notepad such convoluted directions to the Bed and Breakfast, I'm certain I'll get lost. More cursing. I round a bend and a sign points me up a steep hill under a canopy of trees. For the next few kilometres, I follow the signs. Bless the considerate owners.

Jean-Paul, the patriarch of the farm, welcomes me heartily, sees that I'm wet and immediately puts on all the heaters in my lodging. I have a downstairs lounge and breakfast table, and upstairs is the bedroom and bathroom. Monsieur brings me biscuits and crackers with jam and honey. He puts Craig in the barn out of the rain and offers me lurid orange fluffy slippers for my wrinkled feet. 'Tres chic,' he grins. For the rest of the afternoon, wearing slippers and a nightgown, I rest in a comfy chair, cosy and warm, watching the rain fall. Jean-Paul, ignoring the showers, works in his garden.

When Jean-Paul's wife, Regine arrives home, she brings an espresso and a honey cake. I take two slices and ask them if they're related to a lady who runs the Chambre d'Hotel at St Florent. In the evening, I dine with Regine and Jean-Paul. Four courses, including local asparagus, baked salmon and a cheese plate with the famous Chavignol cherve from just upstream. We finish with an apple tarte. I learn about Jean-Paul's past work in South America and Regine asks me about my family. After a week on the road, it feels like I'm among friends. Days like these make me want to be nowhere but right where I am.

Accommodation: Coquelicot, le Petit Plessis, Saint-Firmin-sur-Loire. Wonderful hosts, charming accommodation, excellent dinner and breakfast, cake and coffee, character-filled location. Wi-fi only available from outside table. Price: E45-60. My score: 18/20

Route tips: There are lots of churches to visit along the route. If you like moats, visit Chateau de Sully at Sully-sur-Loire. The Eurovelo 6 winds along riverside paths and detours to ruins and through farmland and forest in this section. The path is quiet, yet there are numerous villages close by.

Distance cycled today: 80km

Actual distance: 64km

What I should have said. 'Madame, would you be so kind as to be my honourary Grandmother?

Chapter Nine

Saint-Firmin-sur-Loire to Pouilly-sur-Loire

Over a huge breakfast, including home-made yoghurt and fresh poached eggs, I do a quick calculation - I've cycled six hundred and seventeen kilometres and am more than half-way across France. It should have only been five hundred and twelve kilometres but I've had a few diversions and experienced the joy of getting lost regularly.

I'm sorry to leave Saint-Firmin-sur-Loire, so enjoyable has been my stay with Jean-Paul and Regine. They come out to the farm gate to wave me goodbye. The day is cool and overcast, even the ducks in the farm pond seem lethargic. I manage a whopping three kilometres before my first stop. But, it's well worth it.

Briare is a town on the confluence of the Loire River and the Canal lateral a la Loire. It's a curious site, a canal flowing over a river via an aqueduct. But what an aqueduct! At six hundred and sixty-two metres, the Briare Aqueduct was the longest navigable aqueduct in the world between 1896 and 2003. Each side of the aqueduct is book ended by two ornamental columns styled on the Pont Alexandre in Paris. It's an elegant and timeless construction, all the more atmospheric and regal with the early morning mist wreathing between the columns. I walk back and forward across its span, snapping photos of the green dragons adorning the columns. There's not a soul about.

For the next few days, the cycle route will alternate between the canal and the river. After a few kilometres cycling on the left bank, I see my first barge, moving at a ridiculously slow putter. The Captain stands high in the cabin, his wife sits on a deckchair in the sun, a scarf wrapped around her neck in the early morning chill. Two bicycles are parked on the bow. Swallows flit over the canal, scooping low to drink. I don't fancy their choice, the water looks green and sluggish. Soon after, a larger barge chugs into one of the hundreds of locks on the canal. The lock master flicks the switch and the lock slowly fills with water, lifting the hulking barge to the correct level. I stop to observe. It's a little like watching a bath-tub fill. Perhaps if someone sprinkled bath salts in?

After Chatillon-sur-Loire, I cycle along a river path of hard-packed gravel and soil. Much of the Eurovelo 6 so far has been on this surface. It makes for easy cycling, but where patches are worn and pot-holed, it can lead to a sore bottom. I kid myself that I'm hardened by the previous six hundred kilometres. Ouch, there's another pothole. At least, Craig has stopped getting punctures. He seems quite content to cruise along beside the river at a gentle eighteen kilometres per hour.

'Look, Craig, terns! Did you know they've migrated all the way from South Africa to feed in the Loire. Imagine cycling that far?'

Craig, wisely, remains mute. Although, at one point, I could have sworn he deliberately aimed for a pothole. I won't mention long journeys aloud anymore. We pass another barge, the captain waves. His wife appears to be asleep in the deckchair. Her head leans back at an uncomfortable angle. The romance of barging seems to consist of standing resolute at the wheel or sleeping. I pedal harder to escape, a boulangerie my target at the next village.

I detour to Neuvy-sur-Loire, not because it's a world-renown town of beauty. In fact, it's singular claim is that a nuclear power station looms on the outskirts of the village. Well, it's a change from chateaus, vineyards and elegant aqueducts! I stop outside the school and read the menu, posted for the information of parents, and nosy Australian cyclists. Today, les enfant are dining on melon, kidneys à la graine de moutarde and a dessert of yoghurt. Tomorrow looks even better - quiche Lorraine, ragout d'agneau, legumes couscous, camembert and cherries. Is that a four-course lunch for school children? Much better than a pie and a packet of potato crisps.

The menu says everything about the French and their relationship to food. From an early age, children learn variety, quality and, perhaps most importantly, the cultural imperative of relaxing over a long meal. Cheese, fruit, eggs, meat... all part of a balanced diet. And cuts of meat such as tripe and kidneys are not only the preserve of old people on a budget. What other western nation would feed their children offal! I study the menu and cannot find any 'low-fat' or 'dairy-free' options. I have yet to see a fat child in France. The proportion of overweight adults is relatively low. When asked how many cheeses in France, my friend Jean-Paul answered simply, 'Three hundred and sixty-five, one for every day!'

The French and their food habits are the perfect answer (antidote?) to a Western diet obsessed with low-fat manufactured meals and magic bullet solutions. They enjoy whole foods, eaten slowly and in the company of friends.

At the turn-off to Belleville-sur-Loire, under the looming towers of the nuclear power station, I cycle past a church from the 12th century. I wonder which structure will remain in the year 2112? The path follows a D road between the river and the canal. I flit between the two water routes, the wildness of the river with sandbanks and half-submerged logs or the quiet of the canal with barges and the trees reflected in the still water.

It's a short, sharp hill climb to Sancerre, a medieval town and wine Mecca for tourists and aficionados alike. Me, I just want lunch. Salade de chevre chaud again, kidneys in mustard sauce, just like the school children, and tarte poire. I quaff a glass of local sauvignon-blanc wine, waywardly overpriced for we tourists. Sancerre is famous for the siege that occurred here in the 16th century Wars of Religion where the Huguenot residents valiantly held out for eight months, no doubt fortified on bread and overpriced wine.

I can report that Sancerre wine does not aid cycling abilities. I wobble around the cobblestone streets, admiring the buildings, the exorbitantly-priced menus and the expansive views of vineyards carpeting the slopes in every direction. A posse of cycle-tourists pull up beside me, outside a wine-tasting cave. The twang of Australian voices jars my ears. I introduce myself and ask how far they've ridden.

'Too far, mate. Up that bloody big hill,' a man replies. They're all riding the same model of 'barge-bike' with a solid frame and wide seat.

'We're barging down the canal. Got bored and decided to come for a ride,' he leans close, 'It's really just an excuse to drink some of the local drop.' With that, they lean their bikes along the stone wall and enter the store.

I ride down the mountain and cruise all the way to Pouilly-sur-Loire. My hand-written directions describe two roundabouts and a narrow lane to my lodging for the night. Yep. Done that. Still no Bed and Breakfast? A woman driving an old Citroen is about to pull out of a bumpy driveway. I wave her down.

'Ou est Chambre d'hote, s'il vous plait,' I ask.

'Why do you ask,' she responds in heavily accented, but clear English.

'I have a reservation,' I respond, wondering what business it is of hers.

'No, not tonight,' she says.

We both stare at each other for a few seconds.

She smiles, 'I am the owner of the hotel. We have no reservations.'

I look around for signs to the Bed and Breakfast. There are none.

'Oui,' I say, 'I have an email.'

She sighs, switching off the car engine and opening the door.

'Please, follow me.' She walks back down the driveway. I follow. We round a garage, with excavation work taking place nearby and enter a lovely garden in front of her house. The Bed and Breakfast. She motions for me to sit on a garden seat in the sun.

'Can you wait here for fifteen minutes, s'il vous plait? I must pick up my daughter from the Gare, then I will return and find you a chambre.'

Fair enough.

True to her word, Anne-Marie returns in a short time and installs me in a downstairs room. She apologises for the mix-up and describes where I can get supplies for the night in town. I cycle back into town, past numerous wineries. I can't resist. I stop at one cave and wait for the fork-lift driving owner to finish parking her load of pallets. Although she can't speak English, she eagerly pours me samples of her wares. Frankly, whenever I sample wines with the vigneron looking on, I feel foolish. What a charade. As if I know what makes a good wine? If I can swallow it without pulling a face or gagging, it's okay by me. I choose a dry white and pay the woman Euro 10.

Back in the garden, Anne-Marie and I share the Pouilly-fume and she tells me what it's like to be the only left-winger in a conservative town. She smiles at the mention of President Hollande.

'Finally, after years of Sarkozy.' She sips contentedly from her glass. As the sun fades, I tell her of my journey so far. The bottle is finished before evening. I'm asleep soon after.

My wine vote?

Pouilly-fume over Sancerre.

Accommodation: Pouillyzotte B&B, rue de Charenton, Pouilly-sur-Loire. Comfortable rooms, sunny garden, friendly English-speaking host. Price: E 42-52. My score: 15/20.

Route tips: The Briare Aqueduct should not be missed, a marvel of elegant engineering and design. The path alternates between canal and river. Don't be concerned about wandering between the two. Sancerre is worth a detour, if for no other reason than the view. Take your own 'taste-test' between Sancerre and Pouilly-fume white wines. There are also numerous Chateau in the region.

Distance cycled today: 77km

Actual distance: 55km

What I should have said: 'You want how much for a glass of wine?'

Chapter Ten

Pouilly-sur-Loire to Decize

Today I'm cycling into the Burgundy region, which is enough of an excuse to drink more wine this evening.

The morning chill is stark, with a headwind. For the first few kilometres, the path sits atop the levee with a commanding view of the Loire. A windmill slowly clanks, crows fly over a ploughed field and an old man tends his garden. I pass a patchwork of stone farm buildings, in one enclosure a peacock preens, his feathers fantail wide. The females ignore him. The next paddock has three donkeys and a herd of llamas. The farmer is diversifying. There's not a person around. I stop at a seat provided for flagging cyclists (moi?) and remove the leggings from my panniers and put them on over goose-bump legs.

After admiring a bulwark of barges (a breadth of barges? a battalion of barges?) at Argenvieres, I become lost, again. I trundle over back roads for an hour, hoping I'll come across the bike path. I don't. Only one solution... to stop at a boulangerie. At Cours-les-Barres, whilst getting cake crumbs over my map, I notice that if I take the D40 north, I can reach Nevers, my lunch destination and shave twenty kilometres off the bike path, which I can't find anyway. I foolishly join one hundred and fifty-eight trucks, twenty-three camper-vans and too-many-to-count cars heading to Nevers.

On the outskirts of town, I find a bike path leading me into the Centre Ville, but not before a detour through the horror show of strip shopping. Warehouse after warehouse covered in garish cinema-size signs trumpeting the latest in cheap fashion, home decor and sportswear. Haughty scowling models gaze down from billboards, their anaemic figures draped in new-season rags. After hundreds of kilometres of cycling past vineyards and alongside the Loire, through villages with stately houses and lovely churches, I've entered a foreign country called the suburbs. After the warehouse shops comes the high-rise apartments with washing fluttering on balconies, battered air-conditioners attached to bedroom windows like rusty warts and brick walls scrawled with graffiti, all surrounded by a treeless wasteland. In the car park, two men work on an old Peugeot, the younger man crawls under the front while the old man shouts instructions. I stand up on the bike pedals, looking back from where I've cycled, hoping to catch a glimpse of the vineyards on the distant hillside. The driver of a bus toots his horn shepherding me forward onto a roundabout. I grit my teeth and pedal faster, seeking the sanctuary of the old town.

And an impressive pile of stone and bricks it is too, set on a hill with houses dating from the 14th to 17th century along narrow streets and lanes. Pride of place is the Ducal Palace, commanding a fine view over sculptured gardens and the Loire. After the noise and mayhem of its suburbs, Nevers seems curiously devoid of people and colour. A museum town to be visited on the weekend. I cycle along the alleyways, but can't find anywhere that looks appealing to eat. Truth is, I yearn to be back among the fields, daydreaming and listening to birdsong. I ignore the hunger pangs and cycle through the outlying suburbs on the eastern side of town, more strip shopping, more furniture warehouses, more drive-through boulangeries. Nevers reminds me of a quote I once read, 'I have seen the future and it is for sale.'

I stop at a petit boulangerie in a village and buy a jambon and fromage sandwich for Euro 2. I produce my map and offer it to the lady behind the counter, hoping she'll be able to show me where the bike path is in relation to where we are. Long sentence that, just to admit I'm lost. She studies the map and is about to point to where we are, when her husband, the baker joins us. She speaks to him in French. I can see him thinking, this person is asking where he is?

He takes one look at the map and points a stubby finger at a town called Sermoise-sur-Loire. He looks at me and smiles, 'tout droit.' Straight ahead. His wife interrupts and they discuss directions, at length. The baker points straight ahead, again, then sheepishly adds, 'gauche, un kilometre.' The wife nods, knowingly. I thank them both and take my leave. Five minutes later, I'm lost. Again. I take a deep breath and decide to forget even attempting to find the bike path, instead choosing the D13, beside the Canal lateral a la Loire. It's a quiet country road of undulating hills and windswept villages. I relax into the afternoon.

At the top of one long slow hill, I see an old man cycling towards me. His racing bike is steel-framed and sturdy. He rides in a distinct bow-legged fashion, like a cowboy on a horse. We crest the hill at the same moment. He nods and lowers his cap, ready for the downhill. After he passes, I stop and watch him sweep down the hill, crouching low, leaning slightly forward, a child once again.

I arrive in Decize, where the Canal lateral a la Loire and Canal du Nivernais meet, to be engulfed by hundreds of townsfolk celebrating market day. The streets are closed to traffic. Stalls and the gathering throng take up all available space. I can barely push my bike through the crowds. Whereas Nevers was in danger of becoming a ghost town, Decize is bursting with energy and colour. Children run among the crowds, teenagers sit in groups at the fountain, old men sip Kir in outdoor cafes and families fill shopping baskets with cheeses and saucisse. The nougat stall has a long line of customers. A lady in a flowing linen dress sits in a stall offering naff sailor t-shirts and white sunhats.

Unwittingly, I have booked the only hotel not in the Centre-Ville. It's located two kilometres north of the town. I cycle out and discover it's closed. The sign, as best as I can decipher, mentions 'ferme pour marche' - closed for the market. And why not. I sigh and cycle back into the maddening throng, take a table at a laneway cafe, eat berry tart and drink coffee. Most markets finish at midday or in the early afternoon. It's four o'clock and this market... no, this festival shows no sign of abating. I'm hoping for fireworks over the Loire tonight.

It's a character-filled hotel, when I finally get in. A lodging for workers with a bar serving beer and pastis, single metal beds with frayed but clean sheets, a bathroom the size of a closet and an old water-grill heater on the wall. The owners are a gruff but helpful couple who have lived here forever. My room, with breakfast, costs a paltry Euro 37. Their restaurant is closed tonight. Yep, on account of the market.

They recommend a modern restaurant a short walk away. It's housed in a renovated old factory and has abstract black and white photographs on the walls and waitresses dressed in white blouses and black skirts. A besuited gentleman, who I assume is the owner, wanders between the tables talking to the customers. I order the three course Formule. First course, this being Burgundy, is snails doused in garlic and oil. Main course is steak and frites, with salad, followed by a rich chocolate pudding for dessert. I sip a beer and survey my fellow diners. A table of brawny men with bulging stomachs and red faces eat steak tartare and drink vineyards of rouge. Their voices get louder and more animated as the evening, and the wine, passes. In the far corner, a middle-aged couple eat in silence. The woman begins a coughing fit that she can't break, hacking embarrassingly into her handkerchief, until she's forced to retreat to the bathroom. While she's away, her partner reaches across and cuts a slice from her steak. When she returns, he touches her shoulder in sympathy. She coughs once and resumes her meal. I order another beer. Outside, it starts to rain, gently.

Accommodation: Bel-Air Hotel, Ave de Verdun, Decize. Small room, wi-fi in the main building, friendly hosts, cheap and cheerful, but located outside of the city centre. Price: E37-40. My score: 13/20.

Route tips: The canal or the river? Both offer quiet back roads and small villages. Nevers is a town chock full of history, including the opportunity to visit the Sisters of Charity, where the remains of Saint Bernadette of Lourdes are on display, if you like that sort of thing. Petrol heads should, of course, burn rubber on the way to Magny-Cours, occasional site of the French Grand-Prix. Decize is located on a relatively quiet section of the Loire, but is deserving of an afternoon visit, preferably when the market is on.

Distance cycled today: 80km

Actual distance: 72km

What I should have said: 'Monsieur, it is very hospitable how the whole town has come out to greet the foreign cyclist. Merci.'

Chapter Eleven

Decize to Paray-le-Monial

It's raining this morning and I have little inclination to circle Decize looking for the bike path, so I pedal east on the D979 and... voila, discover the only D-road in Burgundy without traffic. Blackberry grows wild in hedges, sheep without overcoats huddle under trees and I crest my first hill of the day. It won't be my last. Let's call them 'folds in the terre,' which soon enough become sharp creases. But the rain buggers off, so I relax into the cycle and let my mind wander.

What is the name of that movie about a drunken writer sleazing around New England? He's forsaken poetry, love and a future until he meets a young woman played by Kelly McGillis. At the end of the movie, he stands on a chair with a noose around his neck... but he starts thinking of a good line for a poem, and another, until he convinces himself there is still hope... and then a dog bounds in and knocks the chair from under him. I spend an hour cycling past green fields and small villages, recalling every detail from the movie, except the title. Such is the preoccupation of a long-distance cyclist.

Bourbon Lancy is a spa town. On the hill is a belfry, church and the small medieval village. It's in perfect repair, a little too neat for my liking. The ornate signs that hang from every shop are quaint, but appear more for the tourist than the local. Well-dressed ladies sit behind counters in shops offering expensive leather shoes, totally unsuited to wearing on the cobblestones outside. Creeper clings to high stone walls and swallows choreograph the sky. I enter my first bike shop of the trip, in curiosity. The owner asks me how far I've travelled. I answer 'l'Atlantique, l'Allemagne.' The owner whistles, impressed. I add, 'lentment.' Slowly. In faltering English, he says, 'It is zee only way.' As I leave he calls, 'bon voyage.'

In the spa quarter, the Grand Hotel is named more in hope than reality. What is it about spa towns that suggests a fading decadent past and a precarious decrepit future? The buildings are regal yet rusty, the spa pools harbour bacteria rather than wealthy tourists, the bars are windswept and faded, the only customers glassy-eyed senior citizens. What was once a pleasurable holiday now seems the last refuge of the dying. The potential customers of these towns are jetting off to Thailand for beachside massages rather than hanging out beside the eau minerale pool. It's a sad lonely elegance. In a melancholy mood, I cycle out of town through an imposing stand of oak trees.

A sweeping downhill returns me to the quiet back road where I marvel at a farm of failed possibilities. An above ground pool stands warped and empty beside a rusting trampoline. A tepee, one side torn and flapping in the breeze is surrounded by scrap metal. Bike frames linger beside the front fence, waiting for two wheels and new riders. The house is shuttered and boarded, the owners have moved on to wilder, more exotic schemes perhaps?

Lunch is pot-luck at a restaurant beside the Loire. No-one speaks English. Once again, I point to the formule menu and let the waitress decide. Entree is pate and a basket of bread, followed by a plate of raw chicken slivers accompanied by salad. I look at the waitress, confused. She smiles and holds up one hand, indicating I should wait. No worries there. I'm hungry, but tucking into raw chicken? She returns with a sizzling stone plate, carried on a wooden tray. She places it carefully on the table, repeating the words, 'Tres chaud!' I get the idea. With a fork, I toss a few chicken pieces onto my very own barbecue. They sizzle and curl. I turn them quickly. The waitress brings an extra basket of bread and a carafe of water. Perhaps she's expecting flames and second-degree burns and wants the water nearby? I settle in for a slow lunch. Dessert is fromage blanc, the silky cheese-milk so beloved by the French.

Digoin is the start of the Canal du Centre, which I'll be following for the next two days. Built in 1792, it links the Lateral canal a la Loire with the River Soane. After over 700 kilometres, I say au revoir to the Loire. In farewell, I cycle twice over the stone bridge, looking down at the slow running water.

The new path is not well signposted, but a joy to ride. Escargot in their dozens slither across the tarmac... at snail's pace. Ouch, sorry. I do my best to dodge them, even though I'll be eating their cousins later in Beaune. An imposing stand of trees line the canal, fisherman with multiple rods resting on poles stare off over the hills. They all nod or offer a wave as I pass. I have yet to see anybody reeling in a fish.

In the 1670's, Margaret Mary Alacoque in Paray-le-Monial, saw numerous apparitions of Jesus, thus establishing the town's status as a stopover for pilgrims seeking forgiveness and/or divine assistance. My hotel room looks over the Chapelle of the Apparition, its butter-coloured stone facade mute in the evening light. Pilgrims pass below my window in the late afternoon, holding candles. I've been to Lourdes in Southern France and Medjugorje in Croatia, both 'apparition towns,' but thankfully Paray-le-Monial avoids the awful commercialism of those places. No glow-in-the-dark Mary or Jesus plug-in lamps here. Just pilgrims slowly circling.

I wander the town in the evening, have yet another bad French coffee in a cafe (more about coffee in a later Chapter). Paray is undoubtedly a wealthy town, there are more shoe shops than boulangeries. The Centre-Ville is a tableau of old buildings with Frenchmen drinking aperitifs in the fading light. I walk to the stream flowing through the village and like an eager teenager, snap photos of myself at arms length with the backdrop of the church reflected in the water. For dinner, I enter an Italian restaurant. Tonight, I am waiting for the miracle of pizza. Like all French pizzas, it's heavy on the cheese, rich and filling, and washed down with a pichet de rosé, s'il vous plait. Later, I recline in bed, unable to move with the weight of pastry in my stomach. The pilgrims still pass by my window. An apparition can appear at any hour, it seems.

Accommodation: Hotel de la Basilique, 18 Rue De La Visitation, Paray-le-Monial. Quality hotel with large rooms, wi-fi, elegant cafe and restaurant, excellent breakfast and a garage for the bicycle. Price E43-62. My score: 16/20.

Route tips: You may be inclined to wander at your leisure from Decize to Digoin, but do not miss the Canal du Centre from Digoin to Paray. It's an oasis of calm. Even if you don't have a bicycle, I'd recommend hiring one for the journey. It's fifteen kilometres between the two towns and you may want to take it in both directions. A path for those of us who enjoy our cycling easy, with scenery. And with a good restaurant at the end.

Distance cycled today: 84km

Actual distance: 76km

What I should have said: 'Monsieur, petit fromage dans le pizza, s'il vous plait?'

Chapter Twelve

Paray-le-Monial to Beaune

Over a substantial breakfast in an elegant dining room, I chat to a well-dressed businessman. He talks about the economy. He finishes his rant with a shrug and the words, 'what l'Allemagne dictates...'

He leaves the sentence hanging, perhaps embarrassed by linking the words Germany and dictate. The recent history of Europe looms over our croissants and yoghurt. He looks at my lycra outfit and asks how long I've been cycling.

'Nearly two weeks,' I answer.

'And how long will you be in Europe?'

'A few months, maybe more,' I shrug. How far can I ride, I think to myself.

He whistles, impressed. I already know the next question.

'You are retired? Or own a company?' he looks at my battered panniers, doubting his own assumptions.

'I write books for children,' I say.

'l'emploi ideal,' he smiles.

'Oui, the perfect job.' I take another croissant from the breakfast array. Tomorrow, or perhaps the day after, I will start thinking of my next children's novel. Today, I eat and ride.

Leaving Paray is a mirror of my arrival, a lovely back road along the canal bordered by trees and sleepy villages. It's too early for my fisher friends. I'm now deep into Burgundy, with hills sloping up either side of the canal, narrow lanes bordered by hedgerows, stone barns, dairy cattle in green fields and a lockmaster sitting outside his office admiring the view. In twenty kilometres, he is the only person I see. How I love the French and their late starts.

Slowly the fisherman appear. A man and his son each cast a line into the centre of the canal, the boy eager, the father lighting a cigarette, knowing they're both in for a long wait. Three men relaxing on camping chairs discuss the one that got away over an early morning coffee. I notice the cars of each fisherman are old and battered. Fishing may not be just a pastime, but a necessary way of gathering food.

The pristine beauty of Burgundy takes a vacation at Montceau-les-Mines, a mining town, as the name suggests, that has fallen on hard times. A hulking building rusts beside the canal, the chutes previously used for loading coal barges now look in danger of falling into the water. The only mining structure still in use is the Museum of Mines.

Just up the road, in the town of Le Creusot, lives Mickael Vendetta, a young man who became a celebrity for a brief period by posting hulky semi-naked pictures of himself on his blog. He was in turn ridiculed and revered, riding the caustic wave of fame all the way to a music deal, advertisements and appearances on the television show 'The Celebrity Farm.' He was described as 'une marchandise dont le contenu n'est d'autre que son propre message publicitaire' - a commodity whose content is nothing other than his own publicity. I think of Madam Ernestine, all the way back at Coutures, and her unwanted celebrity achieved through writing vibrant entertaining and pithy letters. It makes me admire her all the more.

It's been fifty kilometres since Paray and I'm starving. I stop at a boulangerie in a supermarket complex and regret it immediately. The brioche is topped with sugar and... lollies, the doughnuts are injected with apple baby food. Globalisation can ruin even the French meal.

As if punishing me for my gluttony, the goddess of cycling, let's call her Veloronique, brings on the clouds, a headwind and the road signs announce 'chasseur deforme'. For the next twenty kilometres, I dodge potholes and bounce along. But, still no cars. The D974 is my new favourite road.

After a short climb to Ecuisses, the locks start appearing every few hundred metres. The lock gates are taller as the canal drops significantly between levels. The frequency of the locks gives me the impression I'm cycling downhill even more than I probably am. My pace quickens. A bar tabac with one lonely man at the outside table nursing his beer, passes in a blur. A Renault wagon is parked haphazardly on the grass, the front window open, a small dog pokes his head out and barks at me. An old lady in wellington boots carries a bucket of water to her front garden.

At St-Berain-sur-Dheume, a marriage is being celebrated in the square outside the church. A vintage Citroen, beribboned, awaits the bride and groom. It seems as if the whole village is standing in the square, ready to celebrate.

A couple cycle past, riding the perfect tandem bicycle, she in front on a recumbent seat, legs stretching forward as she pedals, he behind sitting upright orthodox-style. If she tilts her head back slightly, she can look at her husband, admittedly straight up his nostrils, but they both appear happy and relaxed as they cycle along. It reminds me of something from an earlier, more jaunty age.

At Chagny, I leave the Canal du Centre and cycle into the vineyard covered foothills around Beaune, the undisputed wine capital of Burgundy. For the next twenty kilometres I cruise slowly along vineyard paths, on the Route des Grands Crus. Hundreds of day tripping cyclists are out, wobbling between tastings at domaines. I'm always amazed at French vineyards with the ancient vines so low and gnarly growing in brittle shale-like ground. How do they get such magnificence from that?

The temperature heads towards summer for the first time on this trip and I stop to rest on an elegant array of garden furniture arranged under a shade tree. The sign reads 'pour les cyclistes'. As I recline on the chair, I'm tempted to reach out and pluck the grapes from a nearby vine, compliments of the Chateau de Pommard. An overweight couple cycle past, their eyes fixed on the Cave ahead, surrounded by Mercedes and Audis. I wonder if I can enter in dusty lycra and ask for a tasting? My eyes droop. Perhaps an afternoon siesta, first.

Beaune is a walled city. The ramparts and moat remain in good condition. I battle the traffic looping around the stone walls, searching for my hotel. It's a kilometre away from the old town on the road to Seurre. The friendly owner lets me store Craig in the old shed, draped in vines, in the back garden, before showing me to my room. It is perhaps the smallest room I've ever stayed in. My bed runs the length of one wall, a tiny bathroom opposite and there's one rack for hanging clothes. My panniers sit awkwardly against the door. I recline on the bed for a few minutes before claustrophobia encourages me to retire to the sun-drenched front bar where the owner offers me an aperitif.

At night, I treat myself to a Burgundy menu. Escargot (my snail friends!) and mushrooms in a broth; Beef Bourguignon; three local cheeses; and one of the simplest, best desserts I've ever had the pleasure to scoff - Poire pochee au vin. As the name suggests, it's one fantail of finely sliced pear poached in white wine, the other fantail in red wine. The emphasis is on the different flavours each wine offers. Fantastic. I have another glass of local blanc to celebrate. And then return to my cubicle.

Accommodation: Hotel Bellevue, 5 Route De Seurre, Beaune. Friendly owners, small rooms, good breakfast, wi-fi, walking distance to town, garage for bicycle. Price E60-70. My score: 14/20.

Route tips: Beaune is not on the Eurovelo 6 route, but is well worth a detour. Plan to stay an extra day to tour the many wineries and stock up on the tastes of Burgundy. The bike paths through the vineyards make this a perfect romantic getaway for couples. Nothing to do but cycle, drink, eat and relax next to the vineyards. I was tempted to stay an extra day myself, but Craig, my bicycle wanted to see Alsace, further east. Prices in Beaune are higher than the surrounding districts. All that history and atmosphere comes at a premium.

Distance cycled today: 105km

Actual distance: 92km

What I should have said: 'Encore un poire pochee au vin, s'il vous plait!'

Chapter Thirteen

Beaune to Rochefort-sur-Nenon

Before Beaune wakes this morning, I cycle slowly through the old town. Craig complains about the cobblestones. The Hotel de Ville has a lovely facade with a bas-relief of a God and Goddess running, he's holding what looks like a jug of wine, she carries flowers. Perhaps she's hoping to exchange fragrance for a flagon?

What is it about the French affection for old-fashioned merry-go-rounds? Beaune has a beauty, red and white barber-shop stripes with little paintings of vineyards above each section. It deserves its place in the town square. Apart from mega litres of wine, Beaune has a number of buildings with distinctively-tiled roofs. The multi-coloured glazed tile concept is thought to have originated in Central Europe, becoming popular in the Burgundy region at the start of the twentieth century. They're so appealing, I don't know why it isn't done more often. Maybe when I return home, I can renovate my corrugated iron?

Outside of town, I cycle through more vineyards as the red-roofed village of Ladoix-Serrigny slumbers. It's too early, even for church bells on this sunny Sunday. Crows circle the grapevines, like the vignerons, waiting for the season.

After wandering for two hours between Grand Cru villages, I finally arrive at Nuits St-Georges where a conga-line of sleepy locals wait outside the boulangerie. Any baker that popular has to be worth trying. The millefeuille I order is an intricate work of art, biscuity layers holding silken custard, topped by a Miro-inspired masterpiece of icing.

I devour it on a bench seat beside a fountain of a naked lady with a very prominent... bottom, holding an umbrella. Water drops from each corner of her parasol and every person walking past smiles. I move my bike to allow an old man to snap a photo of our naked heroine, sans velo.

In the Foret Domaine de Citeaux, I walk in among the trees until I'm surrounded by greenery. The only sound is birdsong. The damp of this place seems to rise from the ground, moss covers the rocks and tree trunks. I shiver.

The next river on this journey is the Saone, wide and gentle with swans regally sailing past. A jaunty barge motors into the main channel from a canal at Pagny-la-Ville and we race each other to St-Jean-de-Losne. Well, I race him. The captain continues to putter along, alternating between steering and reading a newspaper.

On the outskirts of town, I round a bend and almost collide with a fellow cyclist. We stop, both apologising. His accent is a curious mix of French and Eastern European. He explains he's from Poland, but lives in Paris. This is his first weekend off work in ages. I look at his mud-crusted bicycle. He notices.

'Do not follow the path,' he says, 'I spent thirty minutes pushing my velo through a kilometre of mud.' He curses in Polish, before looking up at the cloudless sky. We both wonder where all that mud came from. We wave farewell and I cycle out onto a road devoid of cars. It's Sunday lunchtime in rural France. No-one wastes time in a vehicle.

At St-Jean, nautical-themed restaurants have pride of place on the waterfront, opposite a collection of working barges and smaller tourist models. I take a table outdoors and, as we're only twenty kilometres from Dijon, order a Porc Dijonnais... I'm guessing mustard cream sauce? Yep. It only takes eight slices of baguette to mop it all up. It's such a lovely day, I break my rule and order a beer, even though I still have forty kilometres to cycle.

At a nearby table, two heavily tattooed men and a woman with pink and black hair and double the tattoos of the men talk to their dog. It looks like an oversized rat and wants to fight every canine that passes. Tattoo lady holds the lead tightly. Without wishing to stare, I try to make out their tattoo designs, but there are so many it's as if they have blue skin. The dog looks at me and growls. He knows what I'm thinking. Strange animals, we humans. Some of us cover our bodies with ink, some ride for one thousand kilometres across foreign countries talking to themselves.

I have dallied too long at St-Jean, admiring the ducks and dogs and swans and swallows. I throw my leg over Craig and cycle unsteadily along the cobblestone street, dodging waiters ferrying beers to the riverside tables. It's such a bucolic day, I almost ride past the turn-off for the Canal du Rhone au Rhin. I try singing to keep myself alert, but can't remember enough words to hold a tune. My Garmin indicates the average speed is slowing considerably. C'est la vie. It is Sunday. The sun is out. I am in the middle of France with a full belly and with little to do but turn the pedals. For two hours, I think of very little but how fortunate I am. Oh yeah, and the possibility of an ice-cream at the next town.

Dole, the town, not the government benefit, is a huge surprise. The birthplace of Louis Pasteur is a water wonderland with the Canal du Rhone an Rhin and its sidepath attracting barges, promenading pensioners, young couples holding hands, families with strollers, cyclists and rollerbladers... scores of rollerbladers. One disco-inspired group are dressed in matching bright orange t-shirts and fawn trousers. One man rolls behind his girlfriend, holding her hips, as if he's waiting for her to whip him past the assembled throng, Rollerblade Derby style. It's all too frenetic and healthy for me.

I stop for an ice-cream and the best salted caramel macaron I've ever eaten. The shopkeeper happily fills my water bottle and asks where I've cycled from. I can never pronounce Saint Nazaire correctly for French ears, so I say 'l'Atlantique.' I hold up my macaron as if it's a prize for such effort. The shopkeeper appears to understand.

Fuelled by all this sugar, I brave the canal path, still cluttered with strollers and rollerbladers. A storm bruises the eastern horizon and it's heading our way. I guess ten kilometres to my hotel for the night? I estimate fifteen minutes until the storm hits. I wish I had a bell to alert the walkers as I race past. The leaves of the stately trees rustle in the wind, shivering from the impending tempest. I am about to get soaked. Don't these walkers see it coming? It's a beautiful canal path, but it offers little shelter. The sign reads three kilometres when the first raindrop falls. I grit my teeth and pedal harder. I can see the church steeple of Rochefort-sur-Nenon ahead. The rain bounces off my helmet. The walkers, as if by magic, have disappeared. It's me and the storm. I lift myself from the seat and pedal with all of my strength. Lightning forks across the eastern sky. I dodge an umbrella, torn and discarded on the path, before rounding a bend and seeing the village through pouring rain. I steer off the path and into the main street. The waitress of the only cafe in town is picking up empty glasses from the outside tables, under umbrellas. I call out, 'l'hotel, s'il vous plait?' She points around the next corner, saying 'gauche' before scurrying indoors.

Thunder rumbles across the village as I reach the door to my hotel. I turn the handle. It's locked. A sign says it opens at five pm, in one hour. I swear, under the front awning. I can't stay here for that long. I quickly cycle back to the cafe and park Craig under a tree. It doesn't shelter my panniers enough from the rain, so I take off my rain jacket and stretch it over the baggage, tying it tight against the wind. I slosh into the cafe. No-one but the waitress and moi. I order a beer, sit at a booth and curse the rain. Craig looks unhappy outside, under the tree.

Eventually, the hotel is opened by a young woman who shows me to my room. I plead with her to turn on the master heater downstairs, that will allow me to dry my clothes in my room. Although she can't speak English, she understands and sets about the task quickly. I appear to be the only guest in the hotel tonight. The window of my room looks out on the deserted street below. The potholes are now puddles.

At dinner, the same woman is the chef, her younger sister is the waitress. I happily devour a three-course meal, content to be warm and dry. The rain has stopped, so I wander the village in the evening.

The cemetery tells me everything about this belle village. The gravestone of Camille Bertin, who died in 1959, one year after I was born, is covered in vases of flowers. The church is small and communal. Rochefort is a beautifully maintained appealing location, just a quick rollerblade from Dole. The population of barely seven hundred citizens delight in a home beside the canal.

On turning for the hotel, I pick up a discarded black vinyl waterproof bag, treasured by we cyclists for keeping our clothes dry in thunderstorms. I could have used that a few hours ago. I shake the water from the bag. Finders keepers.

Accommodation: Logis Fernoeux-Coutenet, Rue Barbiere, Rochefort-sur-Nenon. Comfortable rooms, free wi-fi, friendly hosts who can cook, quaint old-world town on a lovely canal. Price: E62-70. My score: 16/20

Route tips: Spend time in Nuits St-Georges, say hello to the naked umbrella lady and the baker. Dole is well worth a visit, but it's hard to pass up a night at Rocheford for its quaint and quiet charm. Ride the canal path between the two towns. It's a delight.

Distance cycled today: 88km

Actual distance: 70km

What I should have said: 'I'll have two millefeuilles, s'il vous plait. Pour mon amie.'

Chapter Fourteen

Rochefort-sur-Nenon to Besancon

In the morning, the rain tumbles down outside my window. Mercifully, today's ride is only sixty kilometres to Besancon. I sit at my desk and imagine how long I can stay in this hotel before the owners need to clean my room. At breakfast, the same young woman as last night serves me croissants and coffee. A few middle-aged men wander in from the street, ordering coffee and sitting at the window table, looking out at the weather.

After one thousand kilometres, with no rest day, I'm exhausted. The rain falls harder. I consult my trusty map again. There are no towns of significance between here and Besancon, only villages. I thank the young lady for such fine food and service and return to my room. I don't mind getting wet, not really, except my feet. I wear mountain-bike shoes, cleated into my pedals and when wet, they squelch, weigh twice as much as usual, and offer no warmth. I go to the bathroom and remove the plastic bag from the rubbish bin. I take another plastic bag out of my panniers. All of my clothes go into the two black dry-bags, one I brought with me and the one I found last night. I return to reception and ask for rubber bands. This takes twenty minutes trying to mime 'rubber band'. Back in my room, I wrap one plastic bag around each shoe and slip the rubber band tight over my ankle. Voila! Waterproof shoes. Or so I hope. I glance in the mirror. I look utterly ridiculous.

The young lady grins widely as she opens the garage door for me to retrieve my bike. She wishes me 'bon voyage' and watches me wobble down the street. With the plastic around my shoes, it's difficult to cleat into the pedals. Craig is ashamed to be seen with me.

The rains relents for a while, as if showing pity. There's no way I'm taking these bags off though. The path alongside the canal is wet and I spend the first hour dodging puddles. The canal is peaceful and deserves more attention than my embarrassed glances. A mother duck leads a dozen ducklings downstream. I can't help but smile. In the shallow sections of the canal, I see huge fish. Yet, for the first day of this journey, I do not pass any fishermen?

As if to accentuate my ridiculous outfit, the rain clears. The morning hangs heavy over the canal, a slight breeze rustles the leaves of trees and the plastic bags on my feet. So far, my feet feel dry, if a little chilled. I relax into the ride. Villages pass, each offering a warm boulangerie. I stop at one to buy a Paris-brest and to humour the locals. My feet scrap on the vinyl floor of the shop, a small puddle forms around me. The woman at the front of the queue insists I get served before her. The owner takes one look at the puddle and readily agrees. I bow and drip and say, 'Merci,' repeatedly. The village has a new idiot.

At lunch, I arrive in Besancon. My Bed and Breakfast room is warm and welcoming. The owner, Claude, is highly amused at my outfit. He readily offers more plastic bags for tomorrow. He shows me up to my room. The bed is covered in fluffy pillows and a designer spread. The bathroom smells of lavender. When Claude leaves, I drape my damp clothes over every available hanging space and have a long shower.

Dressed in pants and a open-neck shirt, with proper footwear, I stroll downhill into the town centre. Besancon is built around the Doubs River and was listed as a World Heritage town in 2008. It's easy to see why. Located in a narrow valley, it's surrounded by seven hills. And yet, despite this topography, it's a remarkably cycle-friendly place. Bike lanes proliferate and there is a bike-hire scheme for tourists and locals alike. The Eurovelo path and the barge canal cut through a tunnel under Mont Saint-Etienne. Earlier, I rode through it twice, just for the experience of cycling beside a lugubrious barge in a tunnel.

Besancon also takes the gong as the 'town under construction.' Everywhere I walk the roads are being dug up, tractors block the footpath, men in hard-hats dig in the mud, policemen direct traffic because the lights have been removed, the Pont de la Republique is closed to traffic, pedestrians manoeuvre around temporary fences.

Despite all this, I like the town. A woman walks down the street unwrapping her Betty Boop doll; a couple I ask for directions follow me slowly in their car to make sure I arrive at the location; a lady in a boulangerie sells me a delightful version of a sausage roll. The sky clears for the afternoon as I walk through the Centre Ville. Young people are everywhere, Crowds of teenage girls laugh and cautiously eye the two handsome young men sitting beside the canal. The men pretend not to notice, yet one man continually ruffles his hair, preening. I order a beer and while away the afternoon watching Besancon fall in love.

In the evening, Claude recommends a restaurant just around the corner. I'm pleased as the Bed and Breakfast is atop a very steep hill and I don't feel like walking up and down. Unfortunately, the restaurant is closed. I curse and slowly head downhill. A few hundred metres further on, I spy a restaurant attached to a large hotel. Single men sit at individual tables eating. I'm a single man in town. And hungry. I walk in to be greeted by a friendly waitress who shows me to a table. I immediately order a pichet de rosé. When she returns, she asks me what my room number is? In faltering French, I try to explain I'm not staying at this hotel. She looks concerned, excusing herself and walking briskly to reception. I pour a glass and watch as she has an animated conversation with the man in a suit behind the counter. After a few minutes, they both shrug and she returns to my table. She explains, as best as I can understand, that this is not a restaurant for the public, but for hotel guests only. I look pained. She smiles and touches my wrist. It has been decided that I can stay and eat my fill for Euro 15. She leads me to the smorgasbord on offer, explaining that I can help myself to the salad bar, the two hot dishes with rice and as many desserts as I can eat. She wishes me, 'bon appetit.'

The array of food on offer, at this luxury hotel by my standards, is mind-boggling. I fill my plate with salad and cuts of salmon, a quiche Lorraine and a duck terrine. The waitress brings me extra bread. I follow this with beef bourguignon, and a delicious pomme tarte for dessert. I can't resist. I return to the buffet for a fruit salad. The waitress smiles indulgently. I sit back and finish my pichet. At every table except one, diners are eating alone. This is a hotel for business people. I imagine the car park is crowded with Citroen C5s and BMWs. I doubt any of these people cycled here. A stylish young woman walks into the restaurant and every man watches as she walks to a table in the centre of the room. She wears a shimmering blue dress, stockings and high heels. She dines alone, rarely looking up from her iPad. The men close to her table chew their food in slow motion. Thankfully, no-one approaches her.

I pay at the reception and return to the buffet to find my helpful waitress, wishing her a bonne nuit. She watches me leave before clearing my table. I wave from the front door. Back in my room, I stack the pillows on the floor. The pile reaches higher than the bed. I sleep soundly.

Accommodation: La Villa Molina, 12 Chemin Francais, Besancon. Welcoming hosts, lovely rooms, free wi-fi, excellent breakfast. On top of the hill, twenty minutes walk from the city centre. Price: E75-85. My score: 16/20.

Route tips: Don't stray too far from the canal and Doubs River. Both offer a lovely relaxing cycle. If you have a car, I'd be tempted to head for Lods, a small village on the Loue River south of Besancon for the afternoon. Sit on the banks and watch the river tumble over small waterfalls. Return to Besancon for the evening and hope the roadworks are finished. Drive up to the Citadel that looms over the town and admire the view.

Distance cycled today: 60km

Actual distance: 48km

What I should have said: 'Claude, avez-vous un autre oreiller, s'il vous plait?'

Chapter Fifteen

Besancon to Montbelliard

Billy Connolly once said, 'There is no such thing as bad weather, only the wrong clothes.' He was referring to Scotland, but as I set out from Besancon with the rain tumbling down and the clouds suffocating the surrounding hills, I can relate to the sentiment. Two jackets and a pair of lycra shorts is not going to keep this rain at bay. I have double the plastic bags around my shoes, compliments of Claude.

There's always one day in any journey where the emphasis is on getting from one location to another, more than on the sights along the way. The bike path is very quiet this morning. I've noticed fewer recreational cyclists since leaving the Loire and the Saone rivers. Now it's only we madmen, pushing out the miles. The Doubs River flows almost imperceptibly. A quiet descends from the surrounding hills, the only sound a tinkle of raindrops on my helmet. In this reverie, I almost miss a deer bounding through the grass in front of me. Young and skittish, he seeks shelter in the woods, his white tail a bouncing apostrophe.

There's a village every few kilometres, as always, but they seem quieter, more introverted, as if retreating into the hills, away from the path. I shake my head. Is it just me and my mood, or the weather, or the closed nature of these hills? The morning unwinds slowly. I feel the hunger pangs earlier, but push on to Baume-les-Dames, where my map indicates a bike shop and the possibility of wet-weather covers for my shoes, instead of these embarrassing plastic bags.

Typically, I discover a boulangerie first. I stroll inside, scraping plastic across the floor. The owner comes out, wearing a scowl and flour-dusted fingers. I issue a cheery 'bonjour.' He barely grunts in reply. That never happens in France. I'm too hungry and wet to turn away and find another boulangerie. I order a local delicacy, three sugar-frosted shortbreads. The cost is Euro 3. I'm stunned, expecting maybe Euro 1.50 for these tiny biscuits. The owner takes my money and returns to the ovens out back. I sit on the only available chair in the shop and quickly eat the biscuits. They taste sweet and flaky. I call 'au revoir' on leaving. No reply.

The bike shop is located in a backstreet in what looks like an old mechanics work shed. The friendly owner sports a rueful smile. He doesn't need to ask what I'm after, he leads me to the shoe covers and offers me a pair. 'Pour la pluie et le froid,' he says. Rain and cold, that sounds about right. I offer him some money... and the used plastic bags. He holds them away from his body as they drip on the floor. Again, the rueful smile. He calls, 'bonne route' as I leave.

The rain stops immediately. The Doubs River and its sister canal roll side by side. Sometimes, the path leads me between the two, so close to each, that I could almost reach down into the canal and scoop a handful of water and toss it into the Doubs. I look down at my waterproof shoe covers. What the hell. I dismount and lean the bike against a tree. I carefully walk to the edge of the canal, tentative on the wet slippery grass. I lean down and cup a thimble-size amount of water in the palm of my hand. It's cold and oily. Standing up straight, I fling the water across the path towards the Doubs. Almost, but not quite.

This display of childishness cheers me up. I practise whistling. When I was a child, I could never whistle or click my fingers. School friends would mock my inability, call me names, whistle loudly in my direction, like I was a dog hard of hearing. I wasn't too upset though. It's not as if whistling or finger-clicking were necessary requirements for becoming popular. I could kick a football better than most at school, so these other shortcomings were forgiven. As a middle-aged man, I can now click my fingers. But I still can't whistle. I dribble.

Ahead on the path, a man walks towards me, behind him a donkey pulling a cart. When the man sees me approaching, he calls to his donkey. I swear the donkey immediately moves to the right, to give me room to pass. We exchange pleasantries, the man and I, not the donkey, although I dearly wanted to see what other words the animal understood. The sign on the cart reads, 'Dieter on tour 2012'.

Isn't it wonderful to know there are people like Dieter around? His ilk are my heroes. They are an antidote to our current condition that demands constant economic growth and endless hours of work for excessive consumerism. Dieter, to a large degree, lives outside of this madness. We seek 'quality of life' too readily through consumerism, while Dieter walks across Europe with a donkey and a cart. As he continues on, I glance back. Dieter is looking up into the trees, searching for animals. I'm sure I can hear him whistling, but perhaps it's the birds?

The rain has stayed away ever since I purchased these shoe covers. At Clerval, I enter a restaurant, packed with the lunchtime crowd. The waitress shakes her head. No spare tables. A man sitting alone sees this and gestures to me that he's finished. I thank him profusely. I gesture to the waitress that this table is free. She shakes her head. I'm not being served in this restaurant, it seems. I doubt that the formule menu is closed as it's only one o'clock. Maybe my bedraggled appearance has finally met with disapproval, not humour. I stand outside the restaurant, unsure what to do. I don't have the language or the inclination to argue my case. It's the first day on this trip, in fact, the first day of my previous three visits to this serene country, that I have met mild hostility. I am genuinely baffled.

I walk down the road to a truck stop restaurant. All the tables are taken. The waitress, a gruff woman wearing an oversized smock and an apron, asks a single diner if I can share his table. He nods and makes room for me. Beside us in this cramped restaurant are two old Frenchman sharing a carafe of red. Both have florid vein-streaked noses. They can't help but look at my lurid green cycle jersey and lycra shorts. They exchange knowing glances.

I eat ham steak, carrots, potatoes and... Brussels sprouts. I'm not refusing anything at this place. The service is brisk and casual. The two men beside our table order another carafe. The man opposite calls for the bill, nods goodbye and pays at the counter. He walks outside and jumps into the rig of his truck. The bill for three courses is Euro 10.

Shortly after Dampierre-sur-le-Doubs, I say goodbye to the Doubs River, its chocolate-coloured waters flow south while I ride north-east to Montbeliard. It's been another one hundred kilometre day and the weariness seems to surround me, like the clouds on the hills. I cruise the narrow lanes of the old town, under the towering monolith of the Chateau Montbeliard, its two towers dating from the 14th and 15th century. In architectural-speak, it's an imposing pile of stone, looking over the confluence of the Lizzaine and Allan Rivers.

My hotel room has a view of the Stadium Auguste Bonal, home of Sochaux Football Club. The stadium is named after its former director who refused to co-operate with the Nazis and was subsequently murdered. Sochaux FC have a defender with the poetically-inspired name of Yaya Banana.

In the evening, I walk into town and wander the cobblestone streets. I'm going through the motions of searching for a restaurant, gazing disinterestedly at the menu outside every likely candidate. Truth is, I'm not very hungry, despite the one hundred kilometres today. Perhaps the accumulation of so many three-course lunches and dinners is starting to tell on me. I spy a chemist shop, still open. On impulse, I go inside. The weighing machine is near the entrance. Fifty centimes. The verdict? Seventy-seven kilos. Minus one kilo for my shoes and clothes and I have gained only one kilo after two weeks of enjoying huge French meals. I smile, thinking of all the Paris-Brests, cafe éclairs, cheese plates, two desserts per day, the bottles of Kronenbourg and pichets de rosé. I stride back to my hotel, purposefully. They are offering a three-course menu for Euro 15. I can't resist. My hunger has returned.

Accommodation: Kyriad Mont Sochaux, 34 Avenue Du Marechal Joffre, Montbeliard.

Chain hotel offering free wi-fi, free parking and a good restaurant. A ten minute walk from the city centre. Good 2-star hotel standard rooms. Price: E60-65. My score: 14/20

Route tips: Your choice today is to cycle along the canal and river or head into the hills. I'd suggest too much climbing for too little reward. The cycle path is quiet and serene. Avoid the 'La Benne Auberge' restaurant in Clavert. They don't appear to like cyclists! Watch a football match at Sochaux, if it's football season.

Cycle tips: Bring a waterproof jacket. A friendly bike shop is at 8 rue Ernest Nicolas, Baume-les-Dames. The path is mainly bitumen and well-signposted. Lots of villages with boulangeries.

Distance cycled today: 105km

Actual distance: 80km

What I should have said: 'Non, Madam, you are mistaken, I do not want to eat in your establishment. I want to use your toilet.'

Chapter Sixteen

Montbeliard to Mulhouse

At breakfast, I meet a Welsh couple who left Saint Nazaire a few days before me. Their destination? The Black Sea, in Romania. I'm hugely impressed... and envious. Although we left the Atlantic Coast only a few days apart, they've experienced rain every day. I've suffered rain twice and hailstones once. Jane reaches for another slice of baguette and proudly shows me the t-shirts she's had printed for their tour. They display a map of the route and, across the back, read 'hello' in French, German, Hungarian, Romanian.

'We normally camp,' Jane says, looking around at the businessman eating solitary breakfasts. 'But with the weather, we thought why not treat ourselves?'

Her husband, Will, interjects, 'Today, it's back to camping, no matter what, our budget isn't...' He winks at me and sneaks a croissant into his debag. I smile. I'd been considering the same manoeuvre. I wish them clear skies for the rest of their epic voyage.

Today, I leave the Franche-Compe region of France and enter Alsace. The path follows the Canal du Rhone au Rhin, which strictly speaking doesn't flow between the Rhone and the Rhine, but it does allow access between tributaries of both major rivers. My fisherman friends are back in force, ever hopeful. Near Dannemarie, a train races past a bus, which in turn overtakes a cyclist who easily cruises past a barge. The old man walking his dog ignores us all.

Retzwiller is a village of modern block-form houses, individually coloured - yellow, mauve, pink, maroon, orange - it's like passing Legoland. Despite the technicolour of Retzwiller, the houses in the Alsace regions are much more austere than those on the Loire. They have a steeper-pitched roof to keep off the snow, much less ornamentation and a certain solidity that implies winter and bleak skies.

At Eglingen, having made quick time this morning, I decide to leave the canal and head into the surrounding hills. A sign points me towards Altkirch, four kilometres south. I join a few trucks and cars struggling up a long slow hill. My panniers weigh down my progress significantly, but it's pleasant to feel such exertion after the ease of the morning. A brickworks welcomes me to the outskirts of town. The lower section of Altkirch is industrial grey, but on the hill, a far more inviting ancient village awaits. I suck it in and pedal onward. Proof that I'm now in a German-influenced region is the name of the town, loosely meaning 'old church' in German. I pass the stone heavy-set church and find a boulangerie for lunch, a jambon and fromage sandwich, followed by a strudel and a drink for the princely sum of Euro 5. I continue south, following what I suspect is a back road to Hirtzbach. The road gets narrower and has more frequent potholes as I climb. Eventually, it peters out into a bush track in the forest. I'm sure Hirtzbach is in this direction so I pedal on. Soon enough, the road returns and drops steeply. I hurtle into Hirtzbach. Both Hirtzbach and Altkirch feature old houses with decorative support cross beams. They look like the builder was making it up as he went. The timber is painted brown, the house green, or mauve, or yellow. I call it kitsch authentic. I cycle aimlessly around the village for a few minutes, admiring the flowering gardens and the orderly houses, before returning to the canal path.

I arrive at Mulhouse early. At a street corner, I study the map, trying to figure out where I am and where my hotel is. A statuesque blonde woman, dressed elegantly, strolls up to the traffic lights. She pushes the button to cross.

I tentatively offer her my map, asking, 'Ou suis-je?'

She smiles, exposing perfect white teeth. In excellent English, she says, 'You do not know where you are?'

I blush.

The traffic light changes for us to cross, but she ignores it and studies my map. Her perfume envelopes. She points a long fingernail at the map, 'This is the tour de l'Europe.' We both look up to the tower looming above us. 'And where are you going?' she asks. Under her spell, I have forgotten the name of the hotel. My hands frantically reach into my panniers, searching for my notepad and the address of the hotel. Her gaze does not wander from me. She appears to be in no hurry whatsoever. I open the notepad, 'Hotel Le Strasbourg.' She smiles, again. I wonder if she smiles most of the time, brightening the day of each person she meets. She shows me where the hotel is on the map, saying simply, 'Voila.' The lights change again and she wishes me 'bonne journee' before striding away, her blonde hair bouncing. I am a middle-aged happily married man. I try very hard not to look at her as she crosses the road. When she disappears into the crowd, I stuff my notepad into the panniers and cycle towards my hotel. The sun comes out from behind a low cloud.

I check into the hotel, as trams run noisily past my window. It's good to be off the bike for the afternoon. I walk into the old town and have a beer at an outdoor cafe on the cobblestones of the Place de la Reunion. The scene before me best represents my time in France. To my left is a market where I have just purchased a strudel for Euro 1. A butcher at a stall is cutting slices of leg ham and offering them to people. There is a line but I leave my beer at the table and join the queue, I can't resist. The slice of ham is smoky and tender. Next to the market is the neo-Gothic splendour of the Temple of St Etienne, a Protestant Church, built in the 19th century but with exotically-coloured stained-glass windows dating from the 14th century. There's a classical music concert scheduled inside for next week. Alongside the church is a merry-go-round, slowly turning, mothers walking beside their children who are sitting on either a beautifully sculptured horse, elephant, princess carriage, motor-bike or biplane. No-one sits on the donkey with the big ears. Didier, where are you? Near my cafe is a row of old buildings housing a chocolatier, a boulangerie, a fromagerie and a few more cafes.

Every outside table is taken, people drinking either kir cocktails, wine or beer. The French are soaking up the pale afternoon sun and enjoying all that food and wine and history.

As is usual, in the evening I wander the old town looking for a suitable restaurant. As we are so close to the German border, most establishments offer schnitzels and sausages, washed down with German beers. The formule menu appears to have disappeared, replaced by single-dish Teutonic food of a stomach-bulging proportion. Perversely, I ignore these pubs and restaurants and select an Indian restaurant upstairs overlooking the square. A few young ladies sit at the bar when I enter. I am early and there are no other customers. A French-Indian waiter takes my order and soon returns with a delicious chicken curry with fluffy saffron-tinged rice. It's one of the better Indian meals I've eaten. The curry is light and spicy, with copious amounts of chicken thigh. I mop my plate with a garlic naan and order a second beer.

It's a long slow walk back to my hotel. The trams clank across the Place de l'Europe.

Accommodation: Hotel Le Strasbourg, 17 Ave de Colmar, Mulhouse. A simple budget-priced hotel close to the city centre offering spacious rooms, wi-fi and a garage for the bicycle. The front rooms may encounter some tram noise. Price: E42-50. My score: 13/20.

Route tips: By all means, wander away from the canal and river into the surrounding hills. South of the path are many German-influenced villages with distinctive houses and muscular churches.

Cycle tips: A bike shop is at 18 Place Concorde. If lost, I'd suggest asking a statuesque blonde woman for directions.

Distance cycled today: 75km

Actual distance: 65km

What I should have said: 'Je t'aime, je t'aime, je t'aime.'

Chapter Seventeen

Mulhouse to Basel

The sun shines on the tram lines of Rue de Colmar as I cycle over the cobblestones. Workers dressed in overcoats against the morning chill hurry between trams stops and office blocks. At the same street corner where I met the blonde woman yesterday, miraculously, she appears again. She is wearing a long camel-coloured jacket over pleated trousers. She sees me and waves enthusiastically. We smile at each other from either side of the road, waiting for the traffic lights to change. When they do, we both awkwardly walk towards each other, stopping briefly in the middle of the road to exchange greetings. I mumble something about finding the hotel easily, she wishes me a pleasant journey. For the next five minutes, I cycle along the path with an inane grin on my face. Joggers and fellow cyclists give me lots of space. And, without the blonde woman to guide me, I get lost. Again.

Last night, I calculated I'd ridden an extra few hundred kilometres on, or off, the Eurovelo 6 in 'getting lost' and the occasional self-inflicted detour. This morning, still in the suburbs of Mulhouse, I bump over a dirt track on the canal beside a huge barge at a loading terminal opposite. A man stands on a plank half-way down the side of the ship, painting it. His grip looks precarious, as if he'd rather fall into the water than continue painting. I cycle on for another hundred metres and reach a wire fence and a locked gate. Merde! Or should that be Scheisse!

I cycle from where I've come and quickly cross a busy road of cargo trucks and vans. Finally, I enter the Foret Domaniale, with a hard-packed dirt path beside the canal. A memorial, with wilted flowers at the base, honours the soldiers who fought the approaching German army here at a vital bridge across the canal. The soil I walk on carries the ghosts of so many dead warriors. It seems the history of this continent is scattered with the remains of invasion, persecution, resistance and resurrection. Every village I've visited in France has a memorial to the fallen, usually in or near the church or the Mairie. At the conclusion of the Second World War, there were over one million French nationals stranded in Germany, mainly as prisoners of war. By the end of June 1945, all but forty thousand had returned to their homeland, no doubt to assist in the building of these memorials, and to begin the long process of forgetting, or not forgetting, depending on what they did in the war.

At Kembs, I ride in a semi-circle around the Le Corbusier-designed control tower for the lock. It's brutally modernist, but I can see the appeal... just. Unfairly perhaps, I blame Le Corbusier and the modernists for the plague of high-rise housing developments on the outskirts of most French towns I've cycled through. After thirty years of habitation, they are festering sores on the landscape, next to the graceful stone buildings ten times their age. I recall the concrete scars around Nevers of a few days ago and shudder.

I'm a few kilometres from Basle, my destination. The east side of the canal is Germany, this side France, up ahead is Switzerland. In today's global economy, the borders seem more fluid, less important.

They can so easily be breached by the power of the dollar or the deutschmark. The signs that define the landscape now are advertising billboards for Ciba Chemicals, Syngenta, and UBS Bank. Basle is a transport and financial hub for the region and hosts an airport that rather perversely is entirely located on French soil. It's all faintly surreal to an Australian who has to fly for hours to reach a foreign country, if you want to label New Zealand foreign. Basel has suburbs in Germany and France.

Before I cross the canal, I stop at a bicycle shop and celebrate reaching my destination by buying Craig a new rear tyre. The owner happily fits it for me and says goodbye in two languages. Before leaving the shop, I give Craig a quick wipe down with a rag. I want him looking his best for arrival in another country. I reach the customs checkpoint for Switzerland almost immediately. They wave me through, no doubt impressed with the shiny bicycle. Around the next corner, just down a side street is yet another checkpoint to cycle back into France. According to Google Maps, my Bed and Breakfast is on the border with France.

At such a crossroads as this, Basel is a dynamic town on the wide Rhine river. It's the only port for land-locked Switzerland, with water traffic up the Rhine to Rotterdam in The Netherlands. Best of all, it has trams with bells, which I always find wonderfully romantic. I cycle along well-marked cycle lanes beside the road, or sometimes on the road, all the way into the city centre. I lean Craig against the window of a backerei. The display entices with strudels and pretzels and wholemeal rolls filled with ham and cheese. I order a roll and apple strudel, sit on a seat in the square, while Craig basks in the sunshine, and we both watch the trams rattle past. I'm tempted to raise one hand in the air and signal the driver to ring the bell again, just for me, but I may get arrested for public lunacy. My hometown of Brisbane had trams for the first ten years of my childhood, before deciding to modernise and switch to buses. Now, the wide streets are filled the sound of honking horns and the smell of exhaust fumes.

I wander uphill to the Munsterplatz and admire the red sandstone Munster Cathedral. Around the corner is a statue of warrior, small in height, with an extravagant beard and a sword. He is a child's impression of a knight from the Middle Ages, all armour and helmet and pointy sword. If only he'd shave off the ludicrous beard. He looks like an extra from a Monty Python skit.

I cycle across the Rhine, being overtaken at regular intervals by students on single-speed bicycles, old ladies on sit-up European-style cycles and delivery guys on racing bikes. Still, no-one wears a helmet. There are endless cycle lanes and I follow them all, so pleased am I to be in this cycle-friendly town. I know of no better way to slowly and thoroughly see a city. Without a bike, I would never have discovered the Brazilian restaurant; the Ethiopian restaurant down a side street; the Turkish cafe, the suburban backerei where I bought a hunk of cake that I could use as a doorstop if I didn't like the taste. I ate it all. Apple and cinnamon.

Although I love everything about France, except the coffee, it's fun to be in a different country. Everyone speaks English, there is a dizzying array of foods to try and, failing that, I can always amuse myself with a fun game of 'it costs how much?' Switzerland is the most expensive country I've ever visited. A coffee is A$5.50. The bicycle tyre was twice what it would have cost in France. A simple meal costs 50% more than France. Cakes are the only item of a similar price. Amusingly, while riding along the canal into Basel earlier, I was confronted by hordes of fat people jogging. Maybe they should raise the price of those strudels!

Eventually, with the light fading, I cycle back to my Bed and Breakfast where I'm welcomed heartily by Cordula, the owner. She wastes no time in showing me upstairs to my room. The facilities include a huge kitchen and a sundeck overlooking France. I am the only guest. I make an espresso and have my first taste of Basler Leckerli, the local biscuit baked with honey, orange peel, cinnamon and spices. Light and sweet. I sit in the sunshine and look west towards France, recalling the past seventeen days of slow gentle travel punctuated by numerous meals. The usual impression people have of the French is that they are haughty and unwelcoming to foreigners. I found the opposite to be true.

From the first day where a businessman I had asked for directions to the correct platform to catch the train to Saint Nazaire, not only stopped and told me, but ended up waiting outside the platform entrance to make sure that I knew this was indeed the correct one. Nearly everyone I met was interested in my journey and how long I was planning on staying in their country. They offered suggestions of places to go, restaurants to dine in, museums to visit.

I decided, over my second espresso and fourth biscuit here in the sun, that those people who had met hostility and indifference whilst visiting France, perhaps were partly to blame. My rules for travelling in France? Simple. Smile, say bonjour, ask a question in their language however badly you speak it, and always address the person as Monsieur or Madam.

If all else fails, find a boulangerie and eat cake.

Accommodation: Bed and Breakfast Bachgraben, AM bachgraben 36, Basel. Friendly hosts, quiet, free wi-fi, excellent kitchen facilities, wonderful supply of breakfast food for you to cook yourself. A few kilometres from the city centre. Price: E75-90. My score: 16/20.

Route tips: It's basically the Canal du Rhone from Mulhouse all the way to Basel. Enjoy the quiet, because the alternative is noisy highways populated by trucks and speeding cars. Once in Basel, use your bicycle to explore the town. Many locals ride everywhere, so you won't be alone.

Cycle tips: There are numerous bike shops in Basel, so if you're continuing your journey along the Rhine, now is the time to stock up on spares. The cost is higher, but the service is friendly. Ride along the east bank of the Rhine, where there's a path next to the water, with lots of cafes to sit and relax. Backereis, not boulangeries, will now provide your fuel!

Distance cycled today: 43km

Actual distance: 38km

What I should have said: 'Je t'aime, je t'aime, je t'aime.' (again!)

PART TWO

cycling up France

Chapter Eighteen

A boy and a hill

Cycling up France? A grammatical heresy by someone who's spent too long in the saddle and not enough time in the classroom? Not quite. Allow me to explain.

When I was thirteen years old, I owned a three-speed Malvern Star bicycle with a banana seat and dragster handlebars. It was painted luminous blue. I rode it every afternoon around my suburb, particularly down to the Sandies, a sand-dredging operation deep in the bush, where mounds of dirt and hollowed-out lakes were the perfect battleground for kids on bikes. Before the mountain bike was invented, with suspension and gnarly tyres, we rode roughshod over hard-packed dirt, up and down hills, and through mud puddles and across shifting sands. Tumbles were frequent. I learned how to fall off as well as how to hold on.

On the cycle home, I'd occasionally detour to Dellow Street. This street was famous for two reasons. Firstly, because a light plane had crashed into a house in the street and we'd all raced around to see the mangled wreck, the wheel of the plane still spinning, the wings twisted and broken. The pilot survived, thankfully.

Secondly, Dellow Street was a monster of a hill. In distance, it was only a few hundred metres, but riding up was a right of passage for every kid with a bike. I ascended it once a week, beginning by cycling in a lazy zig-zag, lessening the pitch, resting half-way. I knew I was cheating. The only way to say you'd really conquered Dellow was to ride straight up, from a standing start. It took me a year of practice before I could manage it. In a Brisbane summer, the sweat would drip from every pore of my body as I battled against gravity and not enough gears. But I made it.

My reward? To turn at the top and race back down, leaning forward over the handlebars, hands poised on the brakes, grinning wildly while hoping the kids who lived on Dellow would pass the word at school that I'd scaled the titan.

I had a vivid imagination as a teenager.

If I yearned to climb Dellow Street when I was young, how could I now resist scaling the heights of the French Alps, scene of so many Tour de France triumphs and losses. I wasn't planning to race up these behemoths like Lance Armstrong and Cadel Evans, but I wanted to cycle slowly and humbly in their wake, to experience that same exhilaration and sense of achievement I felt in climbing Dellow when I was thirteen years old.

Only recently, I'd ridden up Dellow again as an adult. It was, as I remembered, short and steep, with a gradient of 22% at one point, but never dropping below double figures. From Dellow to Alpe d'Huez is a long serious ride. Up!

Chapter Nineteen

Every cyclist needs their coffee

Before the mountains, let me digress for a moment to discuss that most important fuel beloved of every cyclist. Coffee. The French do most things better than the rest of the world. Food, wine, style, clothes, cars - all memorable and exceptional. But coffee escapes their natural artistry. Particularly in the capital.

Paris - the Louvre; Notre Dame; sidewalk bistros; Sacre Coeur; Pere Lachaise; that chocolate-coloured tower they were supposed to dismantle in 1909; the Seine; the worst coffee in the world... hang on, that last one doesn't fit the script.

I have never had a good coffee in the City of Light. I once saw a barista boil the life out of a jug of milk, put it in the fridge for a few minutes and then scald it all over again. Every cup I've consumed, I've added copious amounts of sugar to 'adjust' the flavour. I've tried espresso, noisette, café allonge, American, latte... all a disaster.

I love Paris. Who doesn't? I love the French, they are friendly, accommodating and slyly humourous. I love French food, what they can do with simple ingredients like butter or flour or cream defies the imagination. But coffee? I'd rather have a cup at the milk bar in Wagga Wagga than risk a Paris cafe.

But, this book is primarily written for cyclists and cycle-tourists, and we all know how much we two-wheel aficionados love our coffee. So, my task today is to locate, for you dear reader, the best coffee in Paris.

Without my wife here, I cannot be expected to stroll over the Pont Neuf, holding hands with myself. I can't linger too long at the Jardin Luxembourg without getting a little teary. I can't eat steak tartare at a sidewalk brasserie. Actually, I can and probably will do that last one. But, a few days prior to my attempts to cycle up numerous French mountains, one could say I need to build up adrenaline for the rigours ahead.

First up, sans mon velo Craig, is managing the Metro, perhaps the best subway system in the world. It's no problem easily and economically navigating my way to the first contestant of today's challenge. Situated in the 4th arrondissement, close to the Seine and Hotel de Ville is La Cafeotheque. Three rooms, a stone's throw from the Seine on the left bank, it has an appealing location and ambience. In the interest of research, I ask the barista what other people are drinking, while pointing at their cups. This unsettles most of his customers, but he answers diligently, 'macchiato,' 'cappuccino,' and 'flat white.' A flat white? It's the first time I've heard that expression outside of Australia, so I order one, double-strength.

The young man brings it to my table on a tray with a glass of water and a chocolate. It's so strong, I have to order extra milk, but it isn't bitter and has obviously been made with Arabica beans, not Robusta, which is what most French cafes persist in using. Quelle horreur!

I relax on a lounge covered in clean hessian coffee sacks admiring the display of coffee beans for sale. The smell of roasting comes from the next room. If you want to hang out somewhere for a few hours close to the centre of Paris, it's a good choice. So,

Cafeotheque scores well in taste, friendly service and location, but loses points for the Euro 5 price tag. That's over $7 for a coffee. Non!

A quick metro transit to the 7th Arrondissement for Cafe Coutume... and it's closed. Merde! Peeking in the window, I see a menu of reasonable priced coffee and an excellent espresso machine and one of those 24-hour slow drip coffee laboratories. So, they're serious about coffee. Pity I couldn't taste it. However, Coutume does lose points for location. It's not somewhere I'd go just for a coffee.

My next step is to ask a semi-local, my son Joe's friend, Jesse, a fluent French-speaking young man of keen intellect and good taste in friends and coffee, studying at the Sorbonne. Jesse walks me through Pigalle in the 9th Arrondissement to KB Cafe, on the way teaching me about conjunctive verbs. Yes, I'm supposed to know that stuff, being a writer and all, but as I suggested, Jesse is smarter than me. I let him do the ordering, at the counter, which in itself is unusual in Paris. No aloof waiters here, just friendly young chaps next to the espresso machine. We're given a table number, which makes me feel like I'm back in Newtown, inner-city Sydney. The coffee is excellent in taste with good crema and is the correct temperature. No burnt milk or tepid coffee here. We share huge slices of carrot cake and raspberry/pistachio cake. The barista doesn't put the last slice of cake back on display either. He cuts it into bite-size pieces and places it on a plate on the counter as a free sample. I like that.

Jesse tells me that, in an earlier life, the cafe was called Kooka Borra Cafe, but recently shortened to KB. The Australian coffee mafia is making inroads, it seems. KB wins in every way - taste, price (E3.50 for flat white), location, being close to Pigalle and Montmartre, and atmosphere - it's a comfortable casual cafe with free wi-fi and tables outside. In fact, I'd rank it as one of the best cafes in Europe I've been to, alongside a cafe in Rotterdam, opened by... yep, an Australian.

Three places in Paris to drink good coffee. That's three more than were here on my last trip in 2010. Go to KB Cafe, if you can. We need to encourage the French to improve the only thing they can't do well.

KB Cafe, 62 Rue des Martyrs, 9th Arrondissement. Metro Station: Pigalle

La Cafeotheque, 52 rue de l'Hotel de Ville, 4th Arrondissement. Metro Station: Pont Marie

Coutume Cafe, 47 Rue de Babylone, 7th Arrondissement. Metro Station: Sevres Babylone.

Accommodation: How many times have you heard that it's impossible to find pleasant friendly accommodation in Paris without paying a fortune? Certainly, many one-star Paris hotels are small, uncomfortable and noisy. In their defence, I'd suggest they are still better than many of the soulless franchise hotels in many large cities.

My suggestion? Try the Sawdays web-site, which offers a list of quirky, interesting places to stay. I have stayed in many Sawdays recommended places throughout France and Italy and found them to be of excellent value and quality.

Chapter Twenty

Col de la Croix-de-l'Homme Mort

I'm not crazy enough to start my mountain adventure by cycling up Alpe d'Huez. First, I'll attempt some 'junior' Tour de France mountains, climbs that should only take me hours and induce endless nausea and vomiting, before I tackle the serious heart-attack summits. And what better mountain to start with than Cross of the Dead Man? Ever since I read about this mountain, I've wanted to cycle to the top.

Appropriately, the day is bleak and cold. The owner of the Bed and Breakfast from last night glumly reports that it's raining everywhere in France except the Cote D'Azur. I'm heading to the mountains of the Massif Central where the Loire River, which I followed across France, begins its long journey to the Atlantic.

Col de la Croix-de-l'Homme Mort has been climbed twice in the Tour de France, first in 1956 and again in 1971. Both times a Frenchman was first to the top. By the time I've unpacked the car and readied myself by eating a cake, the rain has relented and I pedal away from Montbrison, a walled town in the Rhone Valley.

Frankly, I'd rather be climbing on my light and agile Roubaix road bike, but it's at home in Katoomba, snug in my studio. Craig, my heavy hybrid, will have to do.

Who you calling heavy? answers Craig.

He's acting a little peeved lately as I haven't been paying him much attention. We cycle through the early morning streets and witness a carnival stage being erected in the square of a small village.

'Look, Craig, they're preparing to celebrate our first mountain climb,' I say, patting his crossbar.

Silence.

'There's a boulangerie opposite the stage,' I note, more to myself than my stubborn companion.

Just what you need, another cake, Craig mutters.

I can see today is going to be difficult in many ways.

The serious climbing starts a few kilometres outside of town. Craig and I turn right and the road steadily heads skyward. Either side of the wide tarmac are hobby farms and stone houses on handsome estates. Apart from a few old Renault farm cars labouring up the hill, it's just the sound of glorious birdsong and Craig squeaking under the effort of too much weight.

The views into the valley and across to the Rhone Alps are spectacular, with the town of Saint Etienne sprawling in the distance. It's the perfect climb to start my mountain adventures, a Category One ascent with a steady 5 to 6% gradient for fifteen kilometres, good road surface and accompanying cows munching in green meadows and wondering why that man cycling past is sweating so much. The corners are long and slow and offer endless vistas. I quickly get into a rhythm and forget about the ominous clouds overhead. Ramshackle huts selling honey and perfume essence are still closed this early in the season.

And then around one lovely sweeping bend comes five motorcyclists barrelling up in duck-flight formation. My muscles vibrate from all that noise. I admire their skill in hefting those big things around, but riding up and down mountains with that much horse-power just doesn't work for me. And what is it about all that leather?

'We'll stick to two legs and lycra, won't we Craig?'

Silence. He's no doubt thinking the addition of a small two-stroke motor would make things much easier than they are at present. We enter the Verrieres-en-Forez where the gradient ramps up to an occasional 10% for the final few kilometres through pine trees to the summit. It's cool, dark and damp and a chipmunk runs along beside me before darting off into the undergrowth.

Voila! The summit!

The word 'col' in French means mountain pass, so the road doesn't stop here, it tumbles over the hill and down into the village of St Antheme in a narrow valley. Craig and I stand proudly beside the summit sign, indicating we're currently 1,163 metres above sea level. Which could be why I'm feeling slightly giddy. I prefer to think of it as nervous exhilaration.

I have climbed a Tour de France mountain and survived. It only took me... quick check of the Garmin... one hour and nineteen minutes to climb fifteen kilometres.

'What do we do now, Craig,' I ask.

Sleep in the meadow grass?

My bicycle is a real slacker sometimes.

A few hundred metres down the other side of the mountain is the Cafe du Roy, unfortunately closed. I would have enjoyed a celebratory drink, even if it's French coffee. Craig and I stand on the summit for a few minutes, admiring the view along the Rhone Valley.

'It's a long way from Dellow Street, Craig,' I say. If only Billy Barlow, Kevin Vincent and the Ridge boys could see me now.

I'm feeling so chirpy and positive after avoiding the rain, the motorcyclists and the curse of the Dead Man, that Craig and I decide to race down the eastern side to Saint-Antheme. Craig moans that this will require a climb back up the mountain before descending to the car.

That's 'Dead Man's Cross' twice, he emphasises.

Too late, I've already started the descent.

After a kilometre, I'm chilled to the bone with the wind howling up the valley. Craig smirks. I don't mind. This wind will be behind us on the return ascent. It's a rollicking, mercifully quick five kilometres drop to Saint Antheme.

In the village square, a sallow youth in jeans and windcheater sits outside the closed tourist office. He smokes a cigarette and watches me cycle slowly along the cobblestones. I park Craig against a wall and sit near the fountain. The only open shop is a cafe. I leave Craig outside, trusting the young man won't steal him. Craig is such a fetching bike, painted flashy red.

Shortly after ordering an espresso, another cyclist enters, wearing full-length leggings and long-sleeve jersey and jacket. Obviously a Frenchman who knows about weather and mountains. I feel underdressed in shorts, jersey and a thin jacket. He has cycled over the Col des Pradeaux, another Tour mountain on the eastern side of the village. He'll return the same way. Like me, a fool who rides both sides of the one mountain.

He wishes me 'bonne continuation' as I admire his slinky green road bike. The youth outside the tourist office lights another cigarette. He cups it in his hand, gangster style. I wonder how long he'll sit there? Craig and I circle the village one more time, admiring the church with its narrow steeple and heavy wooden door, before taking a collective deep breath and attacking the climb back up Cross of the Dead Man.

On the descent, I hadn't noticed that the gradient was quite so steep. My muscles have cooled and a cramp is working its way along my right leg. I read somewhere that climbing isn't only about leg strength, but is an extended exercise in controlling your breathing. I'm wearing a heart rate monitor that indicates my heart is currently pumping at 152 bpm. I prefer to climb between 130 and 150. I focus on regulating my breathing, letting my legs rotate slowly and steadily. Sure enough, my heart rate drops to 140 after a few minutes even though I'm still pedalling up hill.

I smile at the sleepiest, laziest herd of cows known. They sprawl in the deep grass of the hillside, facing the weak sun, chewing... with their eyes closed! It's a holiday camp for bovines. To complete the postcard image, a stream rushes down from the summit and wildflowers polka-dot the fields. Heart rate now 130. Happy cows, happy cyclist.

It's a short five kilometres back to the summit. Just before the cafe, still closed, I notice an old metal cross near the road. It's overgrown with long grass and stands on a concrete slab with worn engraving that I can't decipher. The real dead man's cross, I imagine.

It's time for the fifteen kilometre descent, enjoying expansive views of the Rhone Valley. Five kilometres down from the summit, I notice a sign pointing to an Auberge. I veer sharply left and follow the lane. The hotel sprawls across a piece of land with commanding views of the plain.

I enter the dining room, a few guests are finishing a late lunch. The waitress greets me and I ask for a chambre for the night. She nods and leads me through the kitchen and out back to a stone building. She shows me a small dark room downstairs. I ask the price. It takes me a few moments to translate. If I'm correct, it's ridiculously cheap.

'Avez vous chambre, regardez vista,' I ask, mixing stumbling French and baby-talk Italian. She nods and leads me upstairs to a much brighter larger room with a deck facing the Rhone Valley. I ask the price. She repeats the same price as the room below. I say 'oui' over and over, to indicate I want this room. She gets the message.

'Velo to voiture, returne.' I really should learn better French. She understands I'll return later with my car.

Outside in the car park, I can't contain my glee. 'Wait till you see the room I've booked us, Craig,' I say. A couple sitting outside wonder why that man is talking to his bicycle. And now he appears to be stroking the seat. They stand and take their glasses inside, just in case.

No matter. Craig and I descend the mountain in a blur, stopping only to celebrate with a tarte d'abricot in Montbrison.

My lease car is a Citroen C3 Picasso. Perhaps the only thing it shares with the famous painter is a confused sense of style. I have folded the back seats down which allows Craig ample room to rest and recover after his exertions. The Picasso is fitted with the latest technology that allows the engine to switch off, momentarily, when stopped at traffic lights, to save fuel. When I take my foot off the brake, it springs into life and lurches forward like a drunk at a bar who's just heard there are free drinks for the next hour. Craig snores from the back seat as I drive back up the twisty mountain road.

After an afternoon sitting on my deck, taking in the delightful views, I enter the restaurant of my auberge. The owner who I met earlier, an older woman wearing an apron and two teenage girls are sitting at a table, eating their meal before the guests arrive. I am too early. Nevertheless, they offer me a table and ask if I'd like to order a drink. Would I ever. I splurge on a bottle of rosé, costing the princely sum of Euro 5. As they finish their meal, the older woman brings me a menu and tries to explain the formule. I understand the entree of salad but am confused by the main course. Chicken with... something? The teenager with the long blond hair giggles and says 'snap, snap' opening and closing her fingers in a scissors motion. 'Lobster,' I suggest. She nods and giggles again. Chicken cooked in lobster sauce, I imagine. How can I refuse? Again, the cost is unbelievably cheap.

First course is a salad of asparagus, tomato, lettuce, an egg and dressing. Simple, but uninspiring. Second course is potato gratin served in a dish big enough for four people, mushrooms and beans and two pieces of chicken cooked in a lobster sauce. The baby lobster is still in the sauce, sitting there red-faced, displeased to be sharing a dish with a lowly chicken. I am confused. Is all this food for me? Or am I expected to just take a serve and allow the waitress to ferry it to the next table for my fellow diners? Surely not? I take a large serve. It's wonderfully delicious. The chicken is tender in a piquant smooth sauce. The potatoes are surprisingly light and tasty. I finish my plate. No-one comes to collect the bowls. It's obvious all this food is mine. I can't resist a second helping. The bottle of rosé slowly drains. I ask for extra bread to mop up the sauce.

For the next course, which I really don't need, the waitress brings a huge wooden serving tray with eleven cheeses arrayed around the central knob. With the extra basket of bread, I'm welcome to eat as much cheese as I wish. I half-heartedly try four cheeses - one goat, two soft ripe white-mould local selections and a hard cheddar. Oh my, this is indulgent.

I need a rest before dessert, so ask for an interlude. I survey the room and the other customers. Four men who look like farmers are sitting at one table and two younger men at another table. All are eating intently, heads down, looking up only to order more bread or wine. It's a simple restaurant, catering to locals. I notice a table is set near the fireplace, with food waiting in bowls. A man I'd seen earlier tending the garden comes in and sits down. He is dressed in overalls and a flannelette shirt.

After an hour, I order dessert, a lovely cherry clafoutis. I wonder if there is anywhere in the world where you can eat so much quality home-cooked food for the price? Perhaps Italy? The equivalent meal in Australia, the USA or the UK would cost three times as much. Actually, you couldn't get this sort of meal in those countries. No restaurant would offer eleven cheeses for diners to eat as much as they want. Or huge bowls of potato gratin and chicken cooked in lobster sauce as part of a basic 'workers menu.' And local wine for a few dollars? Sadly, not in my country. In fact, I splurged on the wine. I could have ordered a 500 ml carafe of rosé for Euro 3.50.

The Chambre d'hote is a wonderful experience of regional French rural life, with simple cooking and cosy accommodation, all for a reasonable price. There is nothing 'designer' or 'cutting edge' about it. Simply put, you eat the way rural French people do. And that, as the advertising cliché goes, is priceless.

I am mind-numbingly full. I thank the waitress and the owner, who is also the chef. We agree on a time for breakfast. I sleep soundly, dreaming of climbing endless mountains made of cheese.

Accommodation: Auberge de Conol, Verrieres-en-Forez, Conol. Friendly staff, ask for a room with a view, wi-fi in the restaurant, exceptionally good value, eat in the restaurant. Price: E27-48. Restaurant Formule Menu Price: E18 My score: 17/20.

Route tips: Start the ride from Montbrison. There are numerous back roads in this region which enables you to plan a circular route if you wish. Consider cycling the Croix, followed by the Col des

Pradeaux, ending in the town of Ambert, which has a perfectly circular town hall.

Cycle tips: According to MapMyRide, the Col is a Category One ride of 15 kilometres with an average gradient of 4.8%. Maximum gradient is 7%. Elevation gain is 742 metres. It's a pleasant morning ride on an excellent road surface with few cars.

Distance cycled today: 48km

What I should have said: 'Fromage! Just what I wanted after chicken and potatoes!'

Chapter Twenty-one

Col d'Oeillon

Would it be surprising to learn that I ate too much for breakfast? Perhaps not. I drove away from the Auberge vowing to return one day, with an empty stomach. Craig continued to rest in the back as we travelled east, skirting the sprawl of Saint-Etienne. Today's climb is the Col d'Oeillon, part of the Rhone Alps. I park the Picasso in the centre of Chavanay, an appealing village a spit away from the Rhone, particularly on a windy day like today. Thankfully, the vent is blowing from the Rhone, pushing me up the start of the hill.

Craig mutters something about a cold night in the back of the Picasso. We begin our ride beside an old stone wall with poppies growing sidewards into my path. I could reach out and pick one, place it in my lapel? It's a tight winding valley climb, with a rushing stream and small plots of grape vines scaling the hill. An old Citroen, uncle of my silly Picasso, is parked beside a vineyard no larger than a suburban block. The crusty farmer snips at the upper vines, a broad floppy hat shielding his face from the sun.

At Pelussin, I stop at a zebra crossing to let a gaggle of schoolchildren cross. I ask the teacher for directions. He shrugs. He has never heard of the Col that looms over his classroom each day. Obviously, he's not a cyclist.

At the next bend two cyclists are consulting a map. They point me in the correct direction. Up that bloody big hill! The Col d'Oeillon is the most easterly peak of the Mont Pilat chain. This side of the range is ruled by a Mediterranean climate. The sweat on my brow agrees. I am cycling, officially, in the south of France.

After Soyere, the gradient increases to a steady 7% for the next ten kilometres, with the road twisting and turning, poking in and out of the forest. At one farmhouse, the chickens roam the road, their feathers blown wildly by the wind, the baby chicks pushed this way and that. It's like a slapstick Funniest Home Videos.

Col d'Oeillon has been climbed four times in the Tour de France, in 1956, 1985, 1986 and 1995. I'd suggest before the Tour graces it again, the local council do some roadworks as the surface is a little patchy. I'd hate to be in a peloton on the descent. The Col is a Category One climb of twenty kilometres, average gradient 5.4%, but this low average is due to the first few and last kilometres being relatively easy.

At the half-way mark, I stop beside a lavoir for a rest. I could use some shade and the wind is becoming increasingly fluky, pushing me up the hill and then wanting to slam me back down. 'Make up your mind,' I mutter. The view is sensational, with the nuclear power station on the Rhone prominent, like a giant carbuncle on the plain. France gets 80% of its electricity from nuclear installations such as this.

Back in the saddle, Craig and I are not alone. With alarming and increasing regularity, we are being passed by men on sleek racing bikes, pushing out the last few kilometres. I give Craig a gentle pat, tell him not to be bullied by those faster younger types, reassure him we'll make it. He answers, rather flippantly, that perhaps I should try pedalling faster. The nearer I get to the summit, the more I relax. We will make it. Not quickly, but most assuredly. I wonder what the view east will be when we reach the top. Will I be able to see Mont Blanc as promised by a guidebook?

At the top, the wind is blowing clouds in front of the communication tower, playing hide and seek. A cyclist stops and takes my photo in front of the altitude sign, 1,233 metres. Off to my left are two service roads, splitting after two hundred metres, each heading to communication towers. One is the Crete de l'Oellion. I take a deep breath and suggest another five minutes of climbing to Craig. He mutters a word unprintable in guide books. Predictably, I choose the wrong turn-off and we cycle for an extra kilometre to be met by a locked gate and increasing clouds. I offer Craig an apology.

We quickly descend back to the altitude sign and wander across to a closed cafe. Actually, it looks more abandoned than closed. Huddling against the south wall, away from the wind, I remove a quiche from my backpack and eat it slowly. The clouds part long enough for me to see the Rhone shining on the plain. On a exceptionally clear day, you can look east and see Mont Blanc, south and see Mont Ventoux. But, today the haze blurs the horizon.

It's very pleasant to have a mountain top to myself, even for a few minutes before the next peloton arrives. Particularly so because I've expended so much energy getting up here. In the last hour, I have not seen a car, only cyclists. I toast we foolhardy souls with the last of my water. In the 1985 Tour, the famous Colombian King of the Mountain, Lucho Herrera, in the polka dot jersey, raced up this mountain, beating the five time Tour legend Bernard Hinault before dropping down the other side into Saint-Etienne to win the stage. I slowly get back into the saddle, wishing I could do a Lucho and hurtle down off the mountain. My fingers are already poised over the brakes.

Do you know a human can grit their teeth continuously for twenty-two minutes? Col d'Oeillon favours me by sending wildlife across my path on the downhill. First, a young deer skittishly leaps across the road. I barely have time to smile before he's gone. Next an eagle swoops low in my path. He looks at me as he floats a few metres above, sees I am too big for prey and funnels skywards on a thermal. Finally, at the farmhouse, the fluster of chicks return, still windsurfing. They are looking quite professional.

I stop at Pelussin for a beer and to give my teeth a rest. The teacher is bringing his children back over the zebra crossing. I hope he's had as satisfying a morning as me.

Back in Chavanay, I sit in the Picasso, trying to decide what to do next. I've challenged myself on two junior mountains and been able to climb them, with Craig, fairly easily. I take a deep breath. It is time for a real mountain. What the French call a 'hors category' climb. Literally, a mountain so steep and long, it is 'beyond' categorisation.

It's time for Mont Ventoux.

Although, I'd originally planned to cycle a few mountains in the French Alps before Ventoux, I'm feeling confident and want to attempt Ventoux early in the season. The Alps can wait for another week.

Craig will be spared the effort of such a climb. For Ventoux and future climbs, I'll need to hire road bikes, light and strong and properly geared, designed for long hours in the saddle heading skywards. I turn in my seat and pat Craig's handlebars. His French adventure is finished.

I drive into Provence and the fields beside the motorway burst into colour at the thought of summer. Sunflowers sway, lavender hunches in purple glory and everywhere the streams run fast and clear. Once again, I marvel at a country that can grow so much wine. It seems as if every spare parcel of land is covered in vines. I have some serious drinking to do to help maintain all these vineyards.

I've stayed at tonight's Bed and Breakfast before, and on that occasion I had trouble finding it. It's an old stone house in a vineyard. Not hard to find in the south of France, surely. Stone houses? Vineyards?

When my wife and I stayed at L'Ecole Buissonniere, I thought John, the English owner was somewhat abrupt and unfriendly. His attractive French wife, Monique was charming, organised and helpful. I talked to her instead. But, like an old leathered shoe, John wore well. He also prepared a delightful expansive breakfast we could eat in the garden, so I forgave him his manners.

This time, John welcomes me heartily and suggests I put Craig in the shed next to his bike. Craig has a companion! I mention that tomorrow, I'm going to tackle Ventoux.

'Oh, I've done that many times,' says John, haughtily. 'From all sides. Done the lot. Cycled the French Alps too. Alpe d'Huez, Galibier, Deux-Alpes. I was a bit younger, mind. Tomorrow, I'm going scuba-diving off Marseilles.'

'So I can get an early breakfast,' I suggest.

He stops, taken aback. He'd planned a daybreak escape.

'I want to tackle Ventoux before the crowds,' I say, 'before the heat.'

John shrugs, 'Okay. Breakfast at seven.' As an afterthought, he adds, 'I did Ventoux in high summer.'

I forgive him, once again. He shows me to my room, in the attic. It has a deep-set porthole window that looks across the vineyard. With thick stone walls and a tiled floor, the room is cool and quiet. I sit on the wicker chair and stare out the window to the surrounding hills. If I should manage to climb Ventoux, actually make it all the way to the top, I guarantee my time will be much slower than John's. I permit myself a smile. When he was younger.

Monique suggests a restaurant in Vaison la Romaine, the nearest town. Inhabited since the Bronze age, Vaison is a tourist Mecca with a Roman bridge over the River Ouveze dating from the first century and a medieval town situated high on a rocky outcrop, a warren of narrow cobblestone streets. I park in the lower town and wander in the early evening, after most of the tourist buses have departed. The swallows are out, as always, writing their distinctive signature across the cloudless sky.

Tomorrow, I'm attempting to cycle up a legendary Tour mountain. It's obvious I'll need lots of fuel, which is why I order the three-course formule menu from La Lyriste restaurant, washed down with a pichet de Provence rosé. I take a table outside under a canopy. It's a balmy evening. My dinner is an asparagus salad, porcini risotto and a simple sticky date pudding, all artfully presented and cooked to perfection. I have discovered my restaurant for the next two nights. By the time I leave it is packed with customers. At a table inside sit John and Monique, with friends. I wish them bonne nuit and amble around the town until darkness falls at ten pm.

I'm glad I can't see Ventoux from this town.

Until tomorrow.

Accommodation: L'Ecole Buissonniere Bed and Breakfast, D75, Buisson, Vaucluse, Provence. Wonderful rooms, excellent breakfast, wi-fi downstairs, garden and outdoor cooking area, perfect location. Monique is a charming host, John is an acquired taste. Highly recommended. Price: E58-68. My score: 18/20.

Route tips: Spend a day, or an afternoon, in Vaison la Romaine, wandering the old town and eating at La Lyriste, 45 Cours Taulignan, Vaison. If possible, hire a bicycle and cycle around the nearby villages. I'd recommend Seguret for the character and atmosphere and Gigondas for the wine. Wherever you wander in this area is worth the exercise.

Cycle tips: Col de l'Oeillon is a Category One climb of 20 kilometres with an average gradient of 5.4%. Maximum gradient is 8.5%. Elevation gain is 1079 metres. While the same category as Croix de la Homme Mort, it is certainly a harder climb. Perhaps, the perfect training ride for Ventoux? Beware of the winds and cycling in the heat of mid-summer. If so, start early and take your own food. The cafe at the summit is unlikely to be open, but there is food and drink available at the town of Pelussin early in the climb. In the afternoon, drive the two hundred kilometres to Vaison and refuel at La Lyriste.

Distance cycled today: 42km

What I should have said: 'Scuba diving in Marseille! Oh, I did that ages ago. As a teenager. Swam right up to a shark. Punched him on the nose. Pah!'

Chapter Twenty-two

Mont Ventoux

The owner of the bike hire store had seen it all before. Hundreds of prospective clients come in every day, lift the road bikes, testing their weight, lovingly running fingers over the shiny carbon-fibre frames or checking the price of the lurid yellow Mont Ventoux jerseys, promising themselves a purchase if they make it to the summit and return unscathed.

In the late afternoon yesterday, I collected my pre-booked Trek Madone with three cogs at the front, ten gears on the rear cassette. That's thirty gears altogether. Should be enough. I asked the owner if there was a discount for two days hire. He smiled, 'You want to do Ventoux twice, we'll make a deal.' His words were encouraging, even if the tone was 'dream on, amateur.' I vowed to keep this shiny lightweight bike away from Craig. No point in making him feel bad.

I'll never kick a football on the hallowed turf of the Nou Camp. Or don running spikes in front of a heaving crowd at Sydney's Olympic Stadium. But, this morning, in a Provencal village, I'm about to cycle up one of the most feared climbs of the Tour de France. My preparation has been three weeks of cycling across France from west to east with Craig, and in the last few days I've climbed two 'junior' mountains of the Tour de France. Oh yeah, and I've learnt the French translation for 'Call an ambulance, quick!' But, with all this, I'm shaking as I park the car in the grounds of the bike rental shop in Bedoin.

The French philosopher, Paul Fournel, said of Mont Ventoux, 'It leads nowhere. It exists only to be climbed.' Fellow philosopher, Roland Barthes was less complimentary, 'The Ventoux is a God of Evil, to which sacrifices must be made. It never forgives weakness and extracts an unfair tribute of suffering.' Lance Armstrong said, simply, 'It's more like a moon than a mountain.'

Visible from one hundred kilometres in every direction, Ventoux rears from the Provence plain like a hunch-backed giant. What looks like snow on the top, is in fact a barren wasteland of scree and rock. If it's a hot day, beware the last few kilometres, where wind speeds of 320 kmh have been recorded. Every day in spring and summer, hundreds of cyclists attempt the ascent from Bedoin, twenty-one torturous kilometres to the summit. In between strained pedal strokes, the riders think of Lance and Cadel and, most of all, Tom Simpson, the British champion who died a kilometre from the summit during the '67 Tour.

My aim today, if I can't make the summit, is to reach Simpson's Memorial, and like many cyclists before me, leave a memento carried up the mountain for our Tom. But first, there's a few kilometres in between. My muscles are twitching with anticipation as I start, well in advance of the hordes who'll be cycling up later in the day.

After an easy kilometre riding out of Bedoin, the climb begins. Almost immediately, a lone cyclist passes me in a blur and I consider tucking into his slipstream. He's forty metres ahead before I decide to save my energy for the last few kilometres. Let's see who's laughing then, Pierre!

The ascent from Bedoin is in three parts. This first section is a lovely easy climb through vineyards and cherry orchards, the trees heavy with fruit. I check my Garmin, my heart is racing above its usual climbing limit but it's excitement rather than exertion, or so I tell myself. Time for the slow breathing exercises I've been practising. Count to ten, forget the pain in the legs, relax the arms, keep the hands loose on the handlebars, breathe normally.

WHATEVER YOU DO DON'T TIGHTEN UP!

Easy.

I take my first drink of water, wondering if I should have brought two bottles. But all that extra weight? I look back towards Bedoin, still sleepy on this sunny Saturday. The cyclist who passed me has disappeared. I check my heart rate. It's steady. I've ridden four kilometres. I reach for the water bottle again, but stop myself.

The second section, let's call it the 'forest of torture' arrives at the next corner. The gradient ramps up to 9% and doesn't drop for ten kilometres. In fact, it regularly nudges 12%, but the stunted wind-blown pine trees offer redemptive shade and I start to relax. A few very early risers are already descending, whirring past at a scary pace. In truth, I'm more nervous about the descent than the climb. My bike, let's call her Madeleine (I'll explain later), is unfamiliar and has slick racing tyres. The only thing slick about me is the sweat on my bald head. Which brings me back to the forest. The difficulty of this section is the long straight stretches. There's no way to fool yourself into thinking the gradient will drop just around the bend. In high summer, the forest is a furnace of parched air, a stretch feared even by Tour veterans.

I love the little white and yellow pillboxes, let's call them 'tombstones' shall we, that list the gradient and the distance to the summit. I should take a photo of one, but I really don't want to stop and break my rhythm.

Who am I kidding. I'm afraid that if I get off Madeleine, I'll struggle to get back on. I haven't had a sip of the water since the first section, but I refuse to drink until I'm out of the forest. I promise myself a gulp at the Chalet, somewhere up ahead. Another cyclist speeds by downhill, his face contorted in a wild grin of ecstasy, or fear. I have tucked a rolled up jacket into my jersey pocket for the expected chill of downhill. In the forest, it's soaked through with sweat from my jersey. Another corner, another stretch of five-hundred metres, still 9%, before another corner. Like an angry customer at a grocery store, it goes on and on, not pausing for breath.

Sooner than I expect, the third section arrives, the final six kilometres from the Chalet Reynard. This is the famous 'lunar landscape' television images of the Tour de France, where the heat seems to radiate from the pale boulders and scree. At first sight, it is truly unearthly. But, I love it, because the gradient drops to a merciful 7% and I actually increase speed, although it's improving from a very low average. At last, there's a view to take my mind off my legs. The meteorological tower on top of Ventoux is also visible for the rest of the climb, so I know just how close I am.

As I pass Chalet Reynard, a bus unloads a bunch of tourists. One quickly takes my photo, the madman on the bike. Secretly, I'm chuffed. And so, begins the madness of the final ascent, where, on three occasions, I have my photo taken by professional photographers, who run alongside me and offer their business card, so I can visit their web-site later and buy the photo. They wish we cyclists a 'bonne journee.'

Suddenly, my attitude changes completely. I'm smiling, my breathing is slow and easy, I even lean back and take a hand off the handlebars, relax into the view. Is that the Mediterranean? Up ahead are a few riders. I appear to be gaining on them. Surely not. I check my Garmin. The gradient remains at a friendly 7%. I'm four kilometres from the summit. Perhaps twenty minutes from climbing one of the most feared mountains in cycling. And then, I start thinking of a puncture. If I got one, what would I do. Cry? Take a deep breath and fix it, knowing I can never pump enough pressure into the tyres for easy cycling. Or would I just push the bike the remaining distance? I try to ignore these thoughts, stare up ahead where the tower looms ever larger. Three kilometres to go. I pass two cyclists, offering a smile and 'tres difficile'. They nod in agreement, too exhausted to speak.

In the final two kilometres, the gradient again ramps up to 9%, as if Ventoux is having the final word. Mercifully, the wind is cooling, rather than threatening. I ride past Simpson's Memorial, attempt a passable impression of bowing my head in deference while pedalling. I decide to visit and pay my respects on the descent. The second last corner is a sweeping left-hander that faces a towering wall of parched rock and scree. In summer the heat would blast from these rocks and baste the cyclist. I look up. Nothing but rock and deep blue sky. At the final hairpin bend, I do what every cyclist before me has surely done. I increase my cadence, just to show I've got something left. Yeah, dream on.

I've made it. I dodge the tourists alighting from a bus and head straight for the Mont Ventoux sign, where a few cyclists patiently wait their turn to be photographed with the altitude marker. A French cyclist takes my photo and I reciprocate. A cyclist arrives every minute. Another tourist bus disgorges hundreds of photo-snapping day trippers and motorcyclists thunder into the car park.

But, let's forget all that and enjoy the view. To my left are the Alps, much closer than I imagined, with many still snow-capped. Directly below me is the snaking road, littered with cyclists, slowly climbing. To my right, a long view south towards the Mediterranean, villages appear as brown-stone dots from this altitude. Behind me is the meteorological tower. Oh yeah, and a lolly stall and sausage stand. I eat the chocolate bar I brought with me. I don't really want to leave, feeling I've earned the right to dawdle and admire Ventoux's majesty.

My time to the top? Two hours and six minutes. Professional riders take one hour, trained amateurs between one hour thirty and two hours thirty, so I'm happy with that. But, frankly, who cares about time when there is that view and a real sense of achievement. I look at the faces of each of the cyclists as they arrive. Do I look like that? A mixture of pride, exhaustion and something... intangible, like someone who's solved a mystery that's been stalking them for ages.

Is it contentment? Or resolution? Whatever, it's fun watching their faces.

Without wanting to, I shrug into my jacket and slowly begin the descent to Simpson's Memorial. It takes less than two minutes. I lean my bike against a snow post and walk quietly up the stairs to the obelisk. I offer a chocolate bar and a small piece of scree brought up from Bedoin. I wanted to bring a bottle of cognac but couldn't find one small enough to fit into my jersey pocket. It's thought Tom had a few sips of alcohol at Bedoin, before the fatal ascent. Like many Tour riders, any drug was welcome. The temperature of Ventoux on that day in 1967 was thought to have reached 50 degrees. Tom Simpson, a World Champion, had fallen off once, just a few metres downhill, before supposedly uttering the now famous words, 'Put me back on the bike.' There's much conjecture about what he actually said, but true or not, his courage drove him forward to just below this memorial where he collapsed again.

The foot of the memorial is decorated with bidons, a cycling cap and rocks. Beside the inscription to his memory are two plaques from his daughters, one in 1997 at the 30th anniversary of his death and another in 2007. They are both very moving and sombre. I walk gingerly down the stairs and look back up to the summit. So close.

It's now peak-hour on the Bedoin ascent, with groups of cyclists huffing and sweating their way to the summit. I'm so pleased I set out early. At the Chalet, gangs of motorcyclists gather in the car park beside Winnebagos and tourist buses. I'm surprised by the crowds. I've been told the Chalet refuses to offer water from the tap to cyclists, they must buy a bottle like everyone else. I take a sip from my bottle. It's nearly empty, but the only exertion I'll be doing in the next thirty minutes is hurriedly applying the brakes.

In the forest section, a few riders are already walking and I'm amazed to see some riding up with mountain bikes and old steel-frame bikes. More courage to them. I had it easy on this Trek Madone. At 11am, I arrive back in Bedoin for a celebratory soft drink. No beer, because on the descent, I've decided to ride out from Bedoin after lunch to the Col de la Madeleine, a small mountain I drove over to get here. As I've dubbed my Trek, Madeleine, she deserves an extra few kilometres.

I go to a bar and order a large coke, with lots of ice. I call my wife to tell her I've climbed Ventoux. I try hard not to blubber across twelve thousand kilometres of phone line. Outside the bar, a posse of cyclists are gearing up for the ride. They laugh and challenge each other to predict the time it'll take to reach the summit. Their accents are English. Just like Tom.

After lunch, Madeleine and I set out easily for the Col de la Madeleine. It's a glorious little road, like a scene from the movie, Jean de Florette. And yes, there is a goat herder who sits under a stunted tree, surveying his goats. I stop at the summit and admire the quiet. It's a beautiful cloudless Provence day. The forecast tomorrow is for more of the same which means I'm going to cycle up Ventoux, from a different side.

In the evening, I sit outside at La Lyriste and eat another delicious three courses. I'd like to tell you what I ate, but I honestly can't recall. My mind was half-way up Ventoux. Tom was beside me, reaching across, offering a bottle of cognac. He winked and told me it was just the elixir for climbing. I took a sip and handed it back. He powered away, into the forest.

Accommodation: L'Ecole Buissonniere Bed and Breakfast, D75, Buisson, Vaucluse, Provence. Wonderful rooms, excellent breakfast, wi-fi downstairs, garden and outdoor cooking area, perfect location. Monique is a charming host, John is an acquired taste. Highly recommended. Price: E58-68. My score: 18/20.

Cycle Tips: From Bedoin, Mont Ventoux is a 'hors category' climb of 21 kilometres with a daunting average gradient of 7.6%. Maximum gradient is 10.7%. Elevation gain is 1610 metres. Whatever season you attempt this climb, I'd suggest starting early to beat the crowds. Take two bottles of water, use sunscreen. And the dazzle of the sun off the scree can be blinding, so sunglasses are essential. Don't push too hard in the forest section, save something for the lunar landscape. On the descent be aware that many cyclists and tourist buses climb this road every day. Don't cut corners. Enjoy the experience. Bonne chance.

Distance cycled today: 60km

What I should have said: 'I understand, Tom. I do.'

Chapter Twenty-three

Mont Ventoux on a Sunday

The climb to Mont Ventoux from Sault is the longest, and easiest, of the three popular ascents. There are two reasons for this. Sault is at a higher elevation than Bedoin and Malaucene, the two other starting villages, so there's less elevation gain to the summit. Secondly, the distance is further and the gradient much less, until the road joins the Bedoin ascent at Chalet Reynard. It's the perfect route for my second attempt. Easier, yet I still get the exhilaration of the final climb from the Chalet when I'll meet all the riders who've slugged through the forest.

There's a market in Sault when I arrive, stalls fill the square, tourists wander aimlessly among the hawkers selling Provence tablecloths and sachets of lavender. The locals shop at the tables selling saucisse and cheese. I park on top of a hill and descend through the town at a furious pace, only to discover I'm heading in the wrong direction. A quick u-turn and climb ensues, as I sheepishly ride through the town once again. Then another downhill and sharp left turn before the fields of lavender rise before me. It's very quiet. The road surface is not as well maintained as the Bedoin route and I keep a keen eye for potholes. Up ahead are two female cyclists. I cruise beside them. One is doing it very tough, the other is hardly puffing. I can't see how this will last. They both smile and wish me 'bonne journee' in a German accent.

A stone farmhouse, disused, with gaps where the windows once were, slumbers in a field of lavender, parked in the garage is a rusted Peugeot. I enter a forest, but unlike yesterday, the trees are tall and offer more shade. I can't help checking my Garmin for the gradient. It seems so easy. Yep. 5%. The perfect Sunday cycle. And yet there are no cyclists descending?

I'm overtaken by a cyclist wearing a red and yellow jersey, followed by a second cyclist, and another. Over the next fifteen minutes, twenty cyclists, in the same colours, ride past. I try to maintain a pace with each, but soon drop away. They are younger, I tell myself. The last cyclist is much older than me. He powers away. I go back to admiring the cool of the forest.

At the Chalet, after twenty easy kilometres, my time is a relaxed ninety minutes. I join the throng puffing up from Bedoin. There are hundreds of Sunday cyclists. I pass a few, realising they've had a much tougher climb than I have. I pull alongside an Englishman and we exchange satisfied grins. A moment later, a Rover with British number plates passes, the driver honking his horn, a woman hanging out the window, smiling and waving.

'My support crew,' the Englishman, named Robert, says. 'It's a little embarrassing.'

We ride alongside each other past the rock and scree.

'I promised myself I'd do this before I got too old,' Robert says. He looks up towards the summit.

'You, me, a million middle-aged men, and a few women,' I add.

Robert laughs. 'Better than playing golf.'

'I used to do that,' I say, 'I can't think of a more boring sport.'

Up ahead, Robert's support crew have parked the car. His wife is crouching low, taking photo after photo of Robert's big day. I drop behind to allow him the spotlight. At the bend, he waits for me to catch up.

'I'm a journalist,' he says, 'I've interviewed many of the Tour riders. No matter how hard a stage they've had, most answer questions, patiently, willingly. Imagine how you'd feel, finishing a two-hundred kilometre cycle and then having a microphone thrust in your face?'

While chatting, I've forgotten to appreciate our climbing effort. We've reached the final bend. I drop behind and let Robert lead up the final climb. Like me yesterday, he powers out of the saddle and puts everything into the last few hundred metres. He pulls away. His wife jumps up and down in the car park. He rides into her embrace. I linger to shake his hand and offer my congratulations.

The summit is even more crowded than yesterday. At the summit marker, I look down the road and see scores of runners jogging steadily up a track beside the bitumen. A loudspeaker encourages them onward and upward. A finishing line tape has been strung across the track, just a few metres below us. A jogger, in shorts and singlet raises his arms as he breasts the tape. He gratefully accepts a water bottle offered to him by an official. The tape is lifted again for the next jogger. Everyone is a winner if he or she ascends by foot.

I don't stay as long at the summit today. The crowds are too pushy, too noisy. Too many tourists are looking for the perfect photo opportunity, in front of the summit sign. I put my jacket on and glide down the mountain. Hundreds of riders are still ascending. This will go on all day and into the evening.

The Sault road is quiet and cool, a joy to descend. I don't see the two women I passed earlier. I hope they made it. Back in Sault, I go into a bar and order a beer and a sandwich fromage and jambon, to celebrate. The only other customers are motorcyclists, heavily dressed in leather and boots. In this heat?

When I return Madeleine to the bike shop, I thank the owner, but refrain from buying the Ventoux jersey. Its lurid yellow screams 'look at me, look at me.'

In the evening, I sit in the garden of the Bed and Breakfast. John tells me how he's cycled up all three sides of Ventoux. Lots of times. When he was younger. He offers me a beer to celebrate. I can't refuse. His dog comes up and licks my hand. John winks and rushes inside, returning with a bottle of clear liquid. 'Try this,' he says. It tastes of orange and coffee and spirits. 'My own concoction,' he says, 'You'll power up any mountain after this.' We have two glasses each.

Cycle tips: From Sault, Mont Ventoux is a 'hors category' climb of 24 kilometres with an average gradient of 4.9%. Maximum gradient is just above 9%. Elevation gain is 1185 metres. The easiest of the three routes to the summit of Ventoux, it is a pleasant climb that includes the iconic 'moonscape' final section. The road surface can be a little patchy, so be careful when descending. Again, it's best to leave Sault early in the morning. There are no cafes until Chalet Reynard.

Distance cycled today: 52km

What I should have said: 'Again! Yes, again!'

Chapter Twenty-four

Alpe d'Huez

The following morning, I load Craig back into the Picasso, bid farewell to Monique and John and set out for the French Alps. Inspired by Ventoux, I now want to tackle a few of the iconic Alps mountains, including Col de la Croix der Fer which was traversed in the 2012 Tour de France.

A few kilometres into the mountains, I pull up beside a rushing stream and buy a kilo of fresh-picked cherries from a stall. They cost a paltry Euro 3. All morning, following the twisting mountain road, I snack on their plump juiciness.

In the mid-afternoon, I arrive at the Bed and Breakfast, just outside of Le Bourg d'Oisans. In summer, the owners, Jean-Louis and Anita host five rooms for cyclists, here to tackle Alpe d'Huez. In winter, the rooms are filled with skiers. Jean-Louis is an instructor at the nearby Les Deux Alpes ski resort. He shows me where to hang Craig for the duration of my stay. Craig, unhappily, joins three gleaming road bikes under the house.

I am in cyclist heaven. The village has three cycle shops, numerous cafes and boulangeries and enough winter clothing stores to kit out an Alpine army. On the outskirts of town, beside the Romanche River is Hotel Cascade, offering rooms and meals and a back deck to relax, order beers and gaze up at the snow-capped mountains rearing out of this narrow valley. I order the Plat du Jour, a hefty lasagne, and discover it comes with an excellent salad for entree and finishes with a bowl of chocolate mousse for dessert. That is one superb Plate of the Day. The owner is an English ex-pat who rides mountain bikes and skies and believes he's found nirvana. I can only agree.

Alpe d'Huez is the most glamourous mountain in French cycling, featuring in nearly every Tour de France since 1976. It draws cycling fans like no other. Half-a-million people cram its slopes and the twenty-one hairpin bends during the race, many of them Dutch, whose riders have a knack of being first up the hill. The winner of the Alpe climb is nearly always a contender for the yellow jersey or the King of the Mountain.

Aware of this symbolism, the authorities have named each of the twenty-one bends after a mountain victor, starting with number twenty-one at the bottom. It's a tad cheesy, but who am I to disagree with millions of cycling fans who count off the bends and the names. I order another beer on the back deck of Le Cascade and think about tomorrow.

The morning is bright and sunny and Anita offers me a huge breakfast. Nervously, I check my gear three times before leaving the Bed and Breakfast a few kilometres south of Le Bourg d'Oisans. I try to relax into the warm-up ride along the valley. Alpe d'Huez looms to my left. I focus instead on the road ahead. I'm pleased there's a bike lane, so I can concentrate on my breathing. Truth is, I'm scared of the first two bends, which are both further apart and steeper than their higher brothers. I drove up the mountain yesterday and my Citroen struggled, so I'm a little apprehensive as I cross the Romanche River and look up. The road resembles a ramp in a shopping centre car park, only one that keeps going. If I was Catholic, I'd cross myself about now. Welcome to 12% land.

I immediately drop to the lowest gear on my new bike, who I've dubbed Monica B, can offer. My speed slows to a crawl. Could I walk quicker? I struggle, unsure whether I can go on. My Garmin tells me I'm less than a kilometre into the climb, my legs scream it's all over. Finally, the first bend arrives. Bonne matin Senor Fausto Coppi, winner in 1952. However as there have been more than twenty-one winners, he now shares naming rights with seven-time winner, confirmed drug cheat and charity tour-de-force Lance Armstrong (2001). Their names stand together, uneasily. The punishing gradient continues to the second bend. I concentrate on looking at the spectacular view of Bourg d'Oisans well below me and the snow-capped mountains rising opposite. I keep telling myself to settle into a rhythm. I rise from the saddle and pump just that little bit harder. Monica B responds, tentatively. She is more nimble, lighter and racier than any bike I've ridden. I only wish she had another front cog.

Second bend, bonjour my Dutch friend, Joop Zoetemelk (1976) and the Spanish winner, Iban Mayo (2003). I permit myself a wry smile. The 2010 football World Cup Final was between The Netherlands and Spain, a hostile affair where the Dutch kicked anything that moved. It seemed so out of kilter with their national character - jovial, quick to laugh, inventive. They did not play the villain role well, and were finally beaten by a Spanish side executing the beautiful game as it should be played. I wonder what Joop and Iban would say?

The thoughts of another sport, less torturous than the one I'm playing right now, gives me a boost and I round the third bend easily and start to enjoy the climb. I even overtake another cyclist, wearing a Sky jersey. Each of the guides I've read suggest utilising the bends to your advantage by building rhythm and slowly counting them down. It helps that the gradient has dropped to a much easier 7% and I can pace myself against other cyclists. I switch into relax-mode and count the bends, slowly. By the time I've rounded number eleven, nodding respectfully to Bernauld Hinault, I feel much more comfortable and alert. It's amusing to read all the messages of encouragement painted on the road by fans, many in Dutch. 'Hup' seems to be the most popular word! Fittingly, before the next bend I'm passed for the first, and only, time by another rider. He's wearing the orange colours of The Netherlands. Hup!

A few kilometres from the top is the Huez village with a lovely little church framed by snow-covered mountains and, as I cycle by, a herd of cows roam the nearby meadow, cowbells tinkling down the valley. From here to the top, alpine flowers dot the landscape and I imagine I'm in a television ad for Swiss chocolate, one where the overweight cyclist wheezes all the way up the mountain before gorging himself on kilos of the finest Swiss delicacy. But enough of that dream. I have... quick check of the sign, eight bends to go. For the first time, I'm sure I'm going to make it and defy predictions of a heart attack.

The final four bends are slightly further apart, but I'm so engrossed in the view across to the mountains and above my right shoulder to the Alpe d'Huez village that Monica B and I barely flinch at the increased gradient.

9%.

Pah! Hup! Sorry, I'm starting to sound like a Dutch Ramones cover band.

Bend Number One, Buongiorno Giuseppe Guerini, is long and sweeping and the gradient ramps up yet again for the final thrust, no... final stagger into the village. I cycle past ski shops, closed for the season and a few cafes, but where is the finishing line? There appears to be no official marker for we amateurs? I slow and call out 'finish' to a few cyclists enjoying a coffee. They point further up the resort. I expect to hear laughter as I push on through the village. Amateur indeed. But, sure enough, confusingly there is a bend number zero. I round this bend, but still no altitude sign. I curse and keep pedalling. Finally, the graffiti on the road ceases and I'm spent. Still, no official marker, but this will do. I pull over into a car park and give Monica B a gentle pat. If only Craig could see this view. Time for some naff photos of moi in front of an Alpe d'Huez road sign, grinning inanely.

Alpe d'Huez is primarily a ski and cycle resort of snowfield chalets and chairlifts and shops selling outdoor wear. In summer, it's overrun by shaven-legged, polka-dot-jersey wearing men, and some women, with obscenely large thigh muscles sitting in outdoor cafes drinking coffee and comparing recent climbs. So I join them, even though I have hairy legs and no bulges anywhere. But, I do have a lurid green jersey.

The record time to the top is held by the legendary Marco Pantani at 37 minutes, 35 seconds. My time? 85 minutes.

I wander into the shop where I hired Monica B yesterday. The owner, Oliver, greets me enthusiastically. I proudly tell him my time. He whistles approvingly. And then his wife goes and spoils it all by telling me Oliver finally beat the one hour mark yesterday. What's twenty-five minutes, I suggest. A bloody lot of climbing, that's what.

I retire to a restaurant and indulge in a burger with fries, washed down with an espresso. Afterwards, I wander the village. Ski resorts are curious places in the off-season. The chairlifts hang quietly over the road, most of the shops are closed, the snow ploughs loiter disused in a green meadow. The air is punctuated by the sound of Dutch laughter. A group of hail-fellow-well-met cyclists are celebrating their climb outside a cafe. Beer glasses line the table. It should make for an interesting descent.

I pull on my jacket, take the leggings from my back pocket and prepare for the descent. The wind chill will be unforgiving. I toast the last of my water bottle to the summit and let Monica B roll. She hugs the corners beautifully and I do my best to hang on. The speed nudges 60 kmh regularly as I continually apply the brakes, too scared to go any faster. The landscape zips past. Hello cows, hello struggling cyclist still climbing, hello stupid car cutting the corner on a tight hairpin! What's the Dutch word for bastard?

Too soon I'm crossing the Romanche River and pulling up outside Le Cascade. A beer or three is in order. I show the owner my photos. 'Look, I've been up there.' He smiles, obligingly. I wonder how many times he's forced to do this every day.

I walk through the village to the boulangerie. Paris-brest. The end to a perfect day. Tomorrow, Col de la Croix de Fer.

Accommodation: Le Petit Catelan, Lieu Dit les Sables, 9 Chemin de Catelan, Le Bourg d'Oisans. Bike-friendly hosts, wi-fi, warm comfortable rooms, big breakfast, a few kilometres from town but an ideal base for cyclists. Price: E75-85. My score: 17/20.

Route tips: Oisans tourism offers an excellent free booklet, listing in great detail, 30 cycle routes in the local area. The booklet comes in many languages and is invaluable in offering simple maps and a history of each route. If only every tourist area so valued their visitors. For serious cyclists, I'd suggest a week in town, allowing you the opportunity to tackle many famous Tour mountains, and ample time to eat at Le Cascade!

Cycle tips: Alpe d'Huez is a 'hors category' climb of 14.5 kilometres with an average gradient of 8%. Maximum gradient is 13%. Elevation gain is 1150 metres. Beware the first two bends, the gradient is steep and unrelenting. Don't let the excitement of attacking the Alpe drain all your energy too soon. Better to slowly complete the first few kilometres and attack in the mid-section, or at the end. Allow the bends to be your friend, count them down as your climb. On descent, beware of cars driven by tourists taking in the view rather than watching for cyclists. Also beware of fellow cyclists speeding past too closely. Don't stop for photos on the ascent, you need to maintain a rhythm to fully appreciate the difficulty of this iconic climb.

Distance cycled today: 40km

What I should have said: 'Hup, hup, hup, hup, hup!'

Chapter Twenty-five

Col de la Croix de Fer

The Col de la Croix de Fer is unlike any other climb in the French Alps. It goes up and down, the road winds through forest then open high meadows, the gradient changes from steep to relatively easy back to steep in the space of a few kilometres... in other words, it's a temperamental bastard. The Croix de Fer is a 'hors category' climb, thirty-one kilometres of trying to find a rhythm when the road varies so dramatically.

All this is good enough reason to indulge over breakfast. Anita is a willing host, loading the table with croissants and baguettes, home-made jams and local honey, all washed down with as much coffee as any tight fitting lycra-clad bladder can hold. It'll be my excuse for frequent stops today while climbing. Jean-Louis wishes me 'bonne chance' as I cycle down the gravel driveway. The sky is cold blue as I cruise along the valley road, a quick wave to the folk at La Cascade. I'll be reporting in there tonight for a few recuperative glasses and perhaps some exaggerated storytelling on how easy I found Croix de Fer?

A few kilometres along the RN91, I turn onto the D526 in Rochetaillee, the road winding beside a snow-melt stream into Allemont. The boulangerie is open on the left, a woman behind the counter serves a long queue. I plan a celebration cake for... quick glance at watch, five hours time? If I'm lucky.

The road turns sharp right and folds over itself with two switchbacks, leading to the Barrage du Verney, the first of two dams I'll encounter today. The road now climbs steadily past a large hydro-electric power station, which also houses a museum charting the history of hydro in France. The gradient increases to 7% and loops into a forest. I can hear the Eau d'Oie river below me, tumbling down the hill. The sight and sound of water is always a calming influence, even when pedalling up a steep incline. Occasionally a stream cascades under the road and plunges into the river on the other side. Ahead of me, the gradient ramps up a notch or two and there are enticing glimpses of snowy peaks.

After an hour, I reach the village of Rivier-d'Allemond. In the centre is a stone memorial to soldiers killed in World War One, stark against the backdrop of snow on the mountains. One cafe is just beginning to open, the waiter hoisting umbrellas over the outdoor tables. He waves as I pass and looks up to the snow-capped mountains, as if encouraging me forward. The road curls uphill into the forest again and then, as if emulating the ghost ride at a funfair, plunges back down into the valley. I lose one hundred metres in elevation in a few minutes of exhilarating descent. The road crosses the river and turns back left, the gradient changing from -10% to 11% in a few hundred metres. My muscles have cramped and gone cold on the furious downhill and now scream in complaint at the effort required to keep the wheels rolling. To my left is a gravel mountain slope with icebergs of snow clinging precariously. If I should sneeze too loudly it feels as if the iceberg will loosen and crash to the stream below. Patches of snow dot the roadside. My muscles warm and I try to gather a rhythm, lost on that worthless descent. This is why the Croix de Fer is so feared by cyclists. It doesn't allow steady rhythmic climbing.

And then, as if a reward for the effort, the road leads to the second dam, the Grand Maison barrage, a wonderful vista of turquoise lake surrounded by mountain peaks. It takes me a few minutes to get my head around a lake at an altitude of 1,500 metres. I stop and have a swig of water, snapping a photo of the mountains reflected on the surface of the lake. On the far bank, two pyramid-shaped green hills are dwarfed by snowy mountains rearing behind them.

As I'm about to get on my bike, a tourist bus arrives and unloads a party of camera-happy snappers. One old man ignores the lake and scenery and walks towards me, his eyes fondling the sleek lines of Monica B. He says something in Italian. I indicate I can't speak the language. He smiles and offers to take my photo, with Monica B, in front of the postcard lake. I stand proud as he snaps. As I mount and slowly cycle onto the road, he applauds quietly, the way a football crowd farewells a player. From then on, I view tourist buses with much more tolerance.

It's hard to adequately describe the last section. It is too beautiful for words. The road winds alongside the lake for a kilometre and I'm pleased there's little vehicle traffic as I'm wandering across the lane, my focus is on the lake and the mountains beyond. Two cyclists pass me and push themselves hard to get ahead. They are chatting as they cycle, but neither turns his head towards the lake. Perhaps this is a weekly ride for them? But even so, with that much beauty on offer?

At the end of the lake, I see the road curl enticingly between green alpine meadows dotted with sheep and stone shepherd huts. Rushing streams, like blue veins, funnel down towards the Barrage. My tempo slows as I relax into the most beautiful eight kilometres I've ever ridden. The pastures of green are sprinkled with wildflowers, the road seemingly cradled in an elongated bowl of steeply-pitched mountains. Imagine Lord of the Rings meets The Sound of Music. I'm now cycling among the snowy peaks I've been yearning to for the past few hours. At any moment, I'm expecting a fairy to appear on my handlebars and sprinkle some more magic dust, so intoxicating is the view. Although, this could be me hallucinating at 2,000 metres!

The gradient doesn't matter anymore, I'm in cycling nirvana. Patches of snow are within touching distance and a cafe appears at the turn-off for Col du Glandon, just five-hundred metres up that side road. I'll visit on the way back. I can see the iron cross (Croix de Fer) a kilometre ahead. Sing, Julie, sing, the hills are alive with the sound of whirring cogs.

Monica B responds by breezily cycling up the last kilometre, the road hugging the green hillside, a slight breeze pushing the wildflowers into a tentative bow at the achievement of we cyclists climbing this high. Too soon, I arrive at the mountain pass and slowly cruise into the car park. In front of me are eleven, count them, eleven snow-capped mountains. Behind are seven more. Beside me, the ancient cross, and a cafe. A few cyclists are having their photo taken in front of the altitude sign. I wheel Monica B to the end of the car park and drink in that majestic view. I lean down and consider kissing her handlebars, make do with a loving pat. I lean her carefully against a rock and sit down. I come from a land of arid dry plains as far as the eye can see and further than the rider can cycle. Our mountains are slight forested hills in the flattest, driest continent on earth. This landscape rearing before me is as alien and awe-inspiring as a visit to Mars. To be able to ride this mountain once a week. Imagine that?

Monica B and I retire to the cafe, sitting outside in the bright sunshine. The waitress brings me a jambon and fromage baguette and I think, 'what a place to work.' In all this beauty, I'd forgotten to check my time for the climb. From the Verney - two hours, twenty one minutes. The best recorded time on Strava - one hour, nineteen minutes. Can I blame all that beauty for slowing me down?

I sit on the terrace in the sun and don't want to leave. I amuse myself, taking endless photos of peaks and admiring the iron cross from all angles. It is an impressive cross, the plinth slowly turning rust red with lichen and age. The cross itself is just an outline of the Christian symbol. I look through it to the mountains beyond. The whole structure tilts back on a slight angle, as if all that wind has taken a toll.

Reluctantly, I shrug into my jacket and begin the descent, but only for a few kilometres before veering right and climbing briefly to the Col du Glandon. In a few days, I'll attempt the ascent of Glandon and Croix de Fer from La Chambre, the way of the Tour de France 2012. At the altitude sign, I look down the road I'll be climbing. It is ferociously steep. Something to look forward to. Like a visit to the dentist.

But, for now, I graciously award the Croix de Fer winner of 'the best kilometres I've cycled in my life Award.' I return to the main road and manage the downhill as slowly as possible, to enjoy it all over again, stopping at the lake and looking back up toward the pass. Maybe I could become a shepherd instead of an author? Ride a bike to herd the flock? I like sheeps! Who doesn't like sheeps! My wife could open a cafe/bellydance school, and correct my bad spelling. I could ride this section in the evening, with the sun on the opposite mountains. In winter, I could cross-country ski? Monica B could live in the shepherd hut, ready for the long downhill on the opposite side to Saint-Michel-de-Maurienne. There are three routes to the summit of Croix de Fer. I could alternate throughout the week. The sheeps would graze as I pedal. My wife would grow to love Monica B as much as I do.

Okay, enough of that. I put on warm gloves, a headscarf and grit my teeth for the descent. One last lingering look back...

Farewell, my love.

The descent is chilling, with the short uphill to Rivier d'Allemont a grind of frozen muscles and sweating brow. The cafe waiter is now busy with customers, everyone enjoying the sun outside, watching the torturous work of a few hardy cyclists. Into the forest, the only sound is of falling water and Monica's cog whirring fast. I clock 60kmh and ease up on the brakes. When I was young, I wanted to descend hills as fast as possible. Now, I prefer to slowly savour the thrill, knowing my effort has earned me the reward of this plunging joy. The two switchbacks above Allemont take a minute and I pedal to the boulangerie. The same waitress from this morning takes my order of a millefeuille. I ask if she has water for my bottle. She smiles and animatedly gestures outside to the cistern on the footpath, smiling, 'l'eau de la montagne.' As she wraps my cake, I go outside to fill my bottle. I can't resist a quick taste. Clear and cold, water of the Gods. 'C'est bon,' I say. She repeats, simply, 'la montagne.'

I sit on a seat in the square, eating my cake and drinking the entire contents of the bottle. A refill is in order. I look back up towards Croix de Fer, the sun glistens off the snow. As if the climb wasn't gift enough, I fill my bottle and perform a discreet toast to la montagne.

Accommodation: Le Petit Catelan, Lieu Dit les Sables, 9 Chemin de Catelan, Le Bourg d'Oisans. Bike-friendly hosts, wi-fi, warm comfortable rooms, big breakfast, a few kilometres from town but an ideal base for cyclists. Price: E75-85. My score: 17/20.

Cycle tips: From Bourg d'Oisans, Croix de Fer is a 'hors category' climb of 37 kilometres with an average gradient of 5.4%. Maximum gradient is 13%. Elevation gain is 1505 metres. Don't think the average gradient makes Croix de Fer an easy climb. There are frequent steep sections and, even worse, a few descents mid-climb, that chill your muscles and force more climbing. Pace yourself in the early forest section and enjoy the last eight kilometres. For me, perhaps the greatest mountain section in the Alps. Leave Bourg d'Oisans early and have lunch at the café on the summit. There are also cafes in Rochetaillee and Rivier-d'Allemont for the celebratory cakes.

Distance cycled today: 72km

What I should have said: 'The hills are alive with the sound of...' (sung in a falsetto voice)

Chapter Twenty-six

Les Balcons d'Auris and the Col de Sarenne

It's a perfect early summer's day in Bourg d'Oisans, so why do I have to go and spoil it by cycling up a bloody big hill. No, Monica B and I haven't had a falling out, but after two 'hors category' mountains, parts of my body are experiencing difficulty doing simple things like walking and sitting. And yet, on my planned 'rest day' I have instead decided to cycle Les Balcon d'Auris, the 'route de la roche', a road not recommended for cyclists who suffer vertigo. Me, I'm just scared of heights.

Constructed in 1902 by engineers masquerading as mountain goats, this is one of the lesser-known climbs in the French Alps, primarily because it has never featured on the Tour de France. Too rocky, too dangerous. Just the place to be on my day off.

The main downside is to reach Les Balcons I have to cycle the first five bends of Alpe d'Huez all over again. It's another warm day and the bends pass in a mind-numbing fog of slow dull pain. At La-Garde-en-Oisans, I veer off the main road and descend through a village of a few houses and gardens. My, that is some view from the farmers shed. Somewhere I have read that the next section is a gentle slope. Non. Non. Non. Unless 'gentle' means 8% in French. I strain along a narrow road, a goat-track of potted bitumen, mercifully shaded by overhanging trees.

At l'Armentier-le-Haut, the road turns left to hug the steep mountain cliff. It's here I fully understand the word Balcon is French for balcony, and this narrow bumpy road is indeed a balcony perched on a cliff edge above the valley. Admittedly a balcony with an 8% uphill lean, but... whoa... so that's what vertigo feels like!

I shakily dismount from Monica B and tentatively walk towards the edge of the road and... gulp... look down. My eyes blur, my knees shake and my stomach churns. I tilt my head away from the drop, bend my knees and crouch behind the woefully inadequate 50cm high 'guard rail' made of crumbling stone. It's a sheer drop to the valley below. I sit on the road for a few moments to calm myself. There is no traffic. No-one is crazy enough to drive on this road.

I eventually work up enough courage to coax Monica B slowly uphill. The Romanche River is directly below me. It's like riding along a 500-metre-high diving board. It is an astounding piece of engineering and as long as no-one drives in the opposite direction, I'm sure I'll learn to love it. For now, I'm cycling on the wrong side of the road, away from the edge.

I suck it in and force myself to the right. Monica B and I get the shakes and start weeping quietly. And then come the unlit tunnels, mercifully short. I look ahead and see the ledge of a road hanging from the sheer cliff. I'm still climbing, but I've forgotten the pain in my legs. Fear overwhelms pain any day.

Finally, after two more ledge corners, the road starts to descend and veer away from the cliff face into high fields of grass and flowers. I let Monica B loose. She seems unnaturally eager to get away from this mountain.

I need a stiff drink. We cruise downhill all the way to Le Freney d'Osians where I stride into a cafe and order a... lemonade, because

I've decided to keep going and take on the Col de Sarenne, a little-used back road to Alpe d'Huez.

Refreshed, I join the busy RN91 for a few kilometres to the Chambon barrage, cycling across the dam wall, enjoying the scene of water cascading into the lake, like an gigantic stormwater drain.

Once off the main road, the gradient increases for the climb into Mizoen, the gateway to the Ferrand valley. The day is warming up. I look ahead to where I imagine the road should be. I can see nothing but cliff face. Perhaps the road circles the mountain and climbs from behind? I cycle through a larch forest and into the sleepy village of Clavans-le-Bas where there's a fountain of cool running water. Perhaps it's not traditional French behaviour to dunk your head in the fountain and shake yourself like a dog, but it impressed the two men sitting outside the cafe. I cycle away, refreshed. A few hundred metres on, I realise with all the head-dunking and spluttering, I'd forgotten to fill my water bottle. Merde! I return to the village and offer the two men an encore performance.

Take two. To my left is a big ugly pile of steep rock that I'm sure there's no way through, to my right the valley. The road has to go around the mountain. Simple. And then the hairpins start and it dawns on me. I keep looking up but can't see the road. A sign appears announcing 'Beware Avalanches.' Now that's something an Australian cyclist doesn't see every day. No chance today, though. The snow has melted. But, at regular intervals, there are rocks on the road, having rolled down from up above. I strap my helmet tighter. That'll stop them.

The road gets rougher and narrower and keeps climbing. Yep, we're going over the big ugly rock. As we climb, the view across the valley opens up to a line of mountains with snow, thick and deep on the peaks of the Massif de Ecrins. It's postcard spectacular and helps me forget the grind. I keep stopping, never good for the rhythm, to take more photos of the mountains and the many bends below me.

At one bend, three motorcyclists are parked, taking photos of the mountains. I struggle past them and stop a respectful few metres away. They speak in German. I look down into the valley and see a cyclist a kilometre back on the road. He's out of the saddle and powering uphill, like a machine. I turn and look uphill. Perhaps there's another two kilometres to the summit. Even with a kilometre head start, he'll beat me to the top. I take a long swig of water, one more photo and gingerly mount Monica B, pushing off unsteadily for the final climb. Suddenly, I hear a whir of gears behind me, the cyclist overtakes in a flash and rounds the next corner. I almost topple off my bike in shock. The three motorcyclists suppress laughter. I shrug. Better to climb under my own power, no matter how unsteadily, than to ride those monsters up this beautiful Col.

Fifteen minutes later, I gently lay Monica B into the lush grass at the summit, before I scramble up a pile of rocks to get a panoramic view across the peaks towards Italy. I'm joined on the escapade by four Dutch cyclists who've cycled here from Alpe d'Huez. Of course. They are laughing like school children at finally having achieved their dream. We snap photo after photo in stupid poses, the mountains as backdrop to our boyishness. Look, Mum, I made it!

It's a pity there's no altitude sign for Col de Sarenne, it deserves one at 1,989 metres. I roll slowly downhill and stop to watch a flock of sheep. Scores of lambs bleat and call for Mother and food. I know how they feel. It's mid-afternoon and I haven't eaten anything apart from a chocolate bar. A German cyclist warns me to watch out for marmots on the descent. I'll be quite happy to eat one, if I see it. The road across the summit undulates, traversing streams and passing an archaeological dig. Twenty workers barely look up at we cyclists passing, so engrossed are they in the search for buried... treasure?

At 3pm, after cycling most of the day, I reach Alpe d'Huez, with the curious sensation of descending to the village, not ascending. I check my Garmin. With Les Balcons and the Col, I've cycled a height gain of 1,985 metres, more than I've climbed in one day before. And today was my 'rest' day. I have climbed another 'hors category' mountain.

But, I'm not crying because of that. Today, I have to return Monica B to the rental shop. I promise to come back next week... surely there's another mountain or two we can climb?

Cycle tips: Les Balcons d'Auris and Col de Sarenne is a 'hors category' climb of 33 kilometres with an average gradient hovering around 5.4%. Maximum gradient is a whopping 14%. Elevation gain is 1985 metres. Les Balcons and Col de Sarenne are both little-used vertigo-inducing roads that present cyclists with unsurpassed views and exceptional climbing. While the road surface can be patchy and potentially treacherous on the descent, I'd recommend this route to everyone who loves to get away from the crowds. A road this close to Alpe d'Huez deserves more recognition. But then again, let's keep it as our secret, shall we?

Distance cycled today: 64km

What I should have said: 'J'adore Monica B''

Chapter Twenty-seven

Col du Glandon

After a week in Italy, out of the saddle, bulking up on pizza and pasta, I am back in the French Alps, once again at the Bed and Breakfast in Le Bourg d'Oisans. I have hired a new bike. It seems the exertions of last week stressed Monica B beyond reason and she's been replaced by a Ridley, a Belgian bike built to withstand the rigours of the cobblestone streets of Flanders. I have resisted labelling the bicycle 'Eddy' in honour of the incomparable Eddy Merckx, winner of Tour de France five times. Yes, he's the only Belgian I know. Instead, I've gone for the highly original moniker of... Ridley. Simple, effective and if in a fog of delirium while climbing a mountain I should forget his name, I only have to look at the insignia.

Today, I drive from Bourg d'Oisans, with Ridley slumbering in the back, to the summit of Col du Glandon. My brilliant idea is to climb from the summit up to Col de la Croix de Fer, where I cycled last week, descend to Saint-Jean-de-Maurienne, ride along the valley to La Chambre and then climb back up to Col du Glandon, taking in some of the route of the 2012 Tour de France. A circuit of seventy-two kilometres, with a Hors Category climb of twenty-two kilometres to finish.

I happily introduce Ridley to the pleasures of the easy four-kilometre climb from Glandon to Croix de Fer. Majestic. Ridley is suitably impressed. He has one more cog at the front, offering me a wider range of gears, although, truth be told, I'm already missing the delicious sportiness of Monica B. How she would love revisiting Croix de Fer.

I'm well aware of the increasing temperature this morning, already at 25 degrees, as I breeze into the car-park at the summit of Croix de Fer. No time for lengthy sight-seeing today. I immediately begin the wild descent, looking right to the valley below and rounding a hairpin bend to be confronted with a herd of cows blocking the road. I dismount and nervously push Ridley through the herd. A few bolshie bovines refuse to move so I sidestep as best I can. I love the bells clanging around their neck, cow music! One lazy cow at the rear refuses to move. She stares straight at me, perhaps mesmerised by my lurid green jersey. I take two steps to the left. She follows. I stop, pushing Ridley ever so slightly towards the cow. I'd rather something between me and those horns. The cow takes a step backwards, confused. She's not the only one. I turn around, hoping for help from one of the cow-herders (cowboys?). They are two hundred metres up the mountain. I lift Ridley and back away towards the grass verge, offering this stupid bovine the whole road. She lets out a long bellow and slowly moves past me. I make a mental note to eat steak tonight at Le Cascade.

Back in the saddle I hit the next bend... and the edge of a fresh cow pat. Oh, the splatter! Merde! For the next ten kilometres, I dodge cow dung, which detracts somewhat from the fantastic view of ski villages, forest and snowy mountains. Aware that the Tour descended this same road, I'm surprised the surface is so bumpy and uneven. I don't mind as I'm only going 30-40 kph. I imagine the peloton does close to double that. It could make for interesting riding. I imagine the cows were moved away to pasture during the Tour.

The descent seems to go on forever. I pass the Col du Mollard turn-off where the 2012 Tour diverted to climb yet another mountain. I negotiate a few tunnels and more potholes and cruise downhill into Saint-Jean. After turning right, I notice a street sign informing me I should be heading in the opposite direction. Confused, I stop outside a grocery store and try to get my bearings. I ask a woman with a shopping trolley. She shakes her head and points back from where I've come. Insistently, I point forward. She shakes her head, again and says, 'Italia!'. I get the message. If I keep following my instincts, I'll finish in Italy not at the Col du Glandon. I do as she suggests and follow the road back, until I see a sign directing me to La Chambre. The road is a National Route along the valley, populated by trucks and fast cars with French, German or Italian number plates. I put my head down and pedal Ridley as fast as I dare.

At La Chambre, I sit in the shade of a tree in the village and eat a sandwich looking up to the ring of mountains, trying to pick which one is Col du Glandon. I don't suppose it's that tiny one in the foreground, to the right? Non. A fellow rider cruises into town having descended the famed Col de La Madeleine. Perhaps, I'll climb that mountain on another trip?

It's midday, I've cycled forty-eight kilometres and the temperature is hovering around twenty-nine degrees. Heaven knows what the Tour riders face in July. Mid-thirties? I ride slowly out of town, through a roundabout, past a row of department stores and finally onto the D927, my road to the summit. After a paltry two kilometres of climbing, I stop at a pub to fill my water bottle and scull a coke, my drug of choice. Take that, Lance!

Back in the saddle, I smile at the familiar yellow pillboxes, announcing the kilometres remaining to the top and listing the average gradient of the next kilometre. It's very helpful, until only seven kilometres into the climb, the gradient ramps up to 10%. I've removed my helmet and strapped it to my handlebars and my cycling cap is soaked in sweat, steadily dripping from the brim onto my Garmin. I count the drops to amuse myself. One every ten seconds. The Glandon is named after a stream that follows the road. I dismount and dip the cap into the snowmelt water. Aaaahhhh. Much of the road is exposed to the elements and the heat blasts off the rock walls and scree. I round another hairpin and arrive at Saint-Colomban-des-Villards, admiring a cemetery on the left with neat well-tended headstones in quiet rows. Further on is another cafe but I resist the urge to stop. I know the road ramps up after this village. Directly above the road in the distance is a lone snow-capped peak. I lift myself from the saddle to stretch my legs. An old lady in a brown knitted sweater walks her small dog towards the cemetery.

Outside of town, I see two young riders ahead of me. Surprisingly, they appear to be going slower than I am. I resist the urge to attack. But, I can't help but gain on them, ever so slowly. Finally, on a very steep section, with the road snaking above a sharp drop to the stream, I'm a few metres behind them when they stop and dismount under a shady tree. As I cycle past, one explains that they're stopping frequently 'because the ride is too easy and we just want to look at the view.' I'll remember that excuse, next time I climb a bastard of a hill like this.

I'm now into the last two kilometres. It's widely regarded as one of the steepest sections in the Tour de France. Looking up, I can see people sitting on the top of this natural amphitheatre, watching we cyclists suffer. It's fantastic. A green grass forum of pain and entertainment. It is without doubt, one of the best venues for watching the rigours of the Tour. It is here that attacks will be launched and the stage will be won, or lost. But, I just want to make it to the summit without collapsing. I have very little energy left to push harder. For the past two kilometres, the gradient has maintained a gut-busting 11%. Ridley is shaking beneath my legs.

With one last effort, I wobble into the car park. Four motorcyclists are having their photo taken in front of the summit sign. I lead Ridley to the thick grass and we both lay down for a long rest. We watch the cyclists slowly ascend. Without exception, they are struggling. I lay back in the long grass, close my eyes to the sun and wait for my breathing to regain a slow steady rate. It's perhaps the hardest climb I've endured. My time from La Chambre? Two hours, twenty-two minutes. Ouch!

Cycle tips: From La Chambre, Col du Glandon is a 'hors category' climb of 22 kilometres with an average gradient of 6.4%. Maximum gradient is 13%. Elevation gain is 1475 metres. A difficult climb that saves the hardest section until last, so go easy at the start. Relax in the forest section, as the last six kilometres is relatively exposed. The road surface is excellent and, mid-week, there are few cars. After battling up Glandon, I'd strongly recommend continuing on to complete the last few kilometres to Croix de Fer. You can always claim you've cycled two mountains in one day! There are cafes at Glandon and Croix de Fer. The one at Croix de Fer offers the best views from the balcony.

Distance cycled today: 70km

What I should have said: 'Merde, vache, merde!'

Chapter Twenty-eight

Col du Galibier

'I will not fail in my work in proclaiming that beside Galibier you are but pale and vulgar beers. There is nothing more to do but tip your hat and salute from well below.'

So said the legendary Tour de France director, Henri Desgranges in 1911, about Col du Galibier. Allowing for the poor translation, I can but only agree with Monsieur Henri, who has a monument in his honour one kilometre from the summit.

The Galibier is an icon of cycling, used by the Tour more times than any other mountain in the Alps. Climbed twice in 2011 to celebrate its one hundredth anniversary of Tour involvement, I'm pleased I've left the 'Giant of the Alps' until last. The summit is a whopping 2,642 metres elevation, and today I'm climbing it from Valloire, an alpine ski village eighteen kilometres down the valley. I should mention, many riders first climb Col de Telegraphe before dropping down to Valloire and taking on Galibier. One Hors Category mountain is enough for me today.

The 1911 Tour winner, Gustave Garrigou, on finishing the climb, declared to the organisers, 'You are bandits!', which no doubt pleased the headline-seeking Monsieur Desgranges.

Today, in glorious sunshine, I cycle out of Valloire and immediately hit a kilometre of 9% climbing. It's a torrid beginning. I pity the riders who've already climbed the Telegraphe. I stop briefly at a boulangerie and grab a pain aux raisins. Not the correct way to cycle up a mountain, but I'm low on energy. Oh, what the hell, any excuse to eat cake!

Surprisingly, I find the monster rather benign today. The weather is calm and clear, with a slight cooling breeze. The streams are gurgling with snowmelt and in front of me always lurks le Grande Galibier, the mountain peak from which the Col takes its name. At 3,228 metres, I'm pleased there's not a road to the top of le Grande!

Yesterday, on Col du Glandon, I was stopped by cows blocking the way. Today, it's sheep, being shepherded across the road and up an impossibly steep incline. They bleat and hop and defecate on the tarmac.

The next few kilometres are some of the most relaxing climbing I've done in France. The gradient hovers between 5% and 7% as the road hugs the hillside and I content myself with leaning back in the saddle and admiring the view. My heart rate barely whispers 100 bpm. I lose myself in the reverie of the past few months, cycling across the breadth of this lovely country and, these last weeks, climbing its most iconic mountains. I'd be more than happy to spend every summer in these mountains, taking every back road to a glorious summit. Forget languid days spent on the pristine white sand beaches of my Australia. Give me a lung-busting climb up a lonely road, with the promise of an unparalleled vista at the summit, where there'll be a cafe offering a jambon and fromage baguette for a few Euros. Heaven.

At Plan Lachat, the road crosses to the other side of the valley. It's here the real climbing begins, with the final eight kilometres along a majestic sweep of snow-capped mountains creating an amphitheatre of epic proportions. My imagination hears opera echoing down the mountainside. Perhaps I'm hallucinating from all the effort, as the gradient has ramped up to a consistent 8% and the hairpins are more frequent. I love the lack of a guardrail. It just adds to the wild untamed nature of the beast, even though I'm scared to cycle too close.

There are more riders than on Glandon yesterday and it allows me to pace myself when I start to flag. On one steep section, I pass a young woman on a steel-framed bike, complete with panniers. I'd like to say I shot past her, but she held my rear tyre for a worryingly long period. Next in the race to the top is a confident cyclist, who as he speeds past me, nonchalantly changes down to a lower gear, just to prove how easy it is. Except, he changes too low and almost stops. I ride past him again before he recovers, with much clanking of gears, and passes me again. I try hard not to laugh out loud. The only real competitor on these climbs is yourself.

As with all great climbs, I don't want this one to end. Every switchback allows me magnificent vistas. About five kilometres from the summit, the snow banks start to crowd the road. They provide a comforting coolness. The mountain ahead looks like a Dalmatian, dotted with patches of snow alternating with clumps of rock.

Near the summit, there's a tunnel for cars through the Col. We cyclists have to go the extra few kilometres over the top. And what a pleasure that is. Two metre high snow banks on the mountain side thrill me to laughter. I've never cycled this high before. It's almost as much fun as kissing my wife after not having seen her for two months. Sorry, personal details getting in the way of a cycling story...

Snowmelt trickles across the road and looking down, I can see the switchback bends, grey tarmac a ribbon through the snow, with the lycra dots of fellow cyclists slowly climbing. Too soon, the summit arrives and I have an unsurpassed view of the Haute Alps… and one hundred cyclists at the altitude sign, waiting their turn for a photo. Many cyclists are ascending from the south slope, having first climbed Col du Lautaret. They earn the privilege of cycling past the monument to Henri Desgranges, but they also have to battle more vehicle traffic. The summit is clogged with cars and motorbikes and cyclists, all eager for a photo beside the sign. I wait my turn before putting on a jacket and gloves for the descent.

The snow banks may have been enchanting on the climb, but as I gather pace on the descent, they offer an icy wind chill and a slippery road surface with snowmelt. I clamp on the brakes, grit my teeth and wish I hadn't written that stuff about no guardrails! Wherever possible, I look up from the next corner to enjoy the hard-earned view, but not for too long.

I tailgate a car for a while. Amusing, but it defeats the purpose of being alone on a bicycle on a mountain. I notice more waterfalls on the downhill run and the wildflowers colour the narrow verge before the drop over the edge. I'm tempted to stop at the Beaufort Fromage Shop to celebrate with cheese made from mountain cows, but the car park zips past before I can decide.

Much too soon, Valloire appears. Time for another cake. This time it's tarte de pommes.

I have tackled a giant and survived. Ridley and I rest at a table with an umbrella shading us from the glare of sunshine off all that snow on the peak of Le Grande Galibier.

Cycle tips: From Valloire, Col du Galibier is a 'hors category' climb of 18 kilometres with an average gradient of 7%. Maximum gradient is 10%. Elevation gain is 1216 metres. For the king of mountains, leave early and take a warm jacket. The road surface is very good, but there are no guard rails, so with melting snow, be extra careful on the descent. Remember, you can't cycle through the tunnel at the peak, but then again, who would want to, with the road above offering such amazing views.

Many cyclists choose to climb Col du Telegraphe as a warm-up which adds an extra 12 kilometres and a 'Category One' climb of 7% gradient. Maximum gradient is 8.2%.

Distance cycled today: 38km

What I should have said: 'I will not fail…'

Chapter Twenty-nine

Lunch in a French restaurant

So ends my French cycling adventure. Two months and close on two thousand kilometres of cycling. I return Ridley to the cycle hire shop, cast a longing gaze over Monica B in the workshop and take my leave. Craig is resting in the rear of the Citroen. We are driving together to Paris where I will board a plane home.

But, not Craig. His French sojourn continues with a sabbatical in a barn at Saint-Firmin-sur-Loire with my friends Jean-Paul and Regine, who have kindly offered to look after him, perhaps teach him some much-needed French manners, until I return in one year. I have decided my next trip will be a ride across Germany, perhaps all the way to Budapest during the next European summer. Maybe I'll even talk my wife into joining me?

At Saint-Firmin, I install Craig in a dry section of a wooden barn, between the hay stacks and the tractor. He barely notices me leaving. Jean-Paul promises to take him on a monthly cycle along the Loire, to keep his chain oiled, his handlebars straight, his tyres pumped. I trust in my friend, Jean-Paul. He has even started addressing my bike as Craig, without raising a quizzical eyebrow.

On the drive to Charles de Gaulle airport, I cannot resist one last French lunch. I pull off the motorway, pay the exorbitant toll and trundle into a village somewhere in Burgundy. It has three restaurants. I choose the one without vintage cars parked outside. Vintage cars, modern prices.

I'm quickly offered a table by the woman working the floor with the help of one young waitress. There are twelve tables, most are occupied by families, young couples or a few elderly people enjoying an aperitif. No French person has lunch without first having a drink.

Each table is covered with a green cotton tablecloth and has a pot plant in the centre, plus two wine glasses and a napkin at each sitting. The waitress immediately brings a basket of bread and a carafe of water. The degustation menu is E19.50 (A$25) for three courses, each course offers me five choices. As I'm in Burgundy, I choose the local dishes - six escargot for entree, beef in pinot noir jus for main course, and for dessert, pear soaked in wine.

I notice each table has also ordered a bottle of wine. I make do with a pichet de rosé for a paltry E4. I'm offered a free appetiser of a thin slice of saucisse on a crust; a puff pastry filled with foie gras; and a thimble full of something that tastes like thick honey wine. It's so delicious, I ask the woman what it is. Her explanation probably gets lost in translation, but I think she says it's merlot wine mixed with honey and cassis. Whatever it is, I'd like to order a barrel of it.

The escargot arrive in a dish with six pods, one for each snail soaked in garlic, butter and parsley. It's like eating essence of garlic! After scoffing the snails, I dip my bread into the remaining liquid. I'd be quite happy to toss the snail and just dip endlessly into this pungent concoction.

The main course is the chef's version of Beef Bourguignon - three hefty chunks of beef in a rich thick red wine sauce with tagliatelle and beans. I'm always a little thrown to see pasta on a

French plate, but it helps me soak up the juices of the sauce, along with the extra bread I've just requested.

After the main course is cleared, I notice a French family enter the restaurant. At the head of the queue are a well-dressed handsome middle-aged couple, followed by two adult children, a man in his twenties dressed in a pale open-necked shirt and crisply ironed trousers. His sister is the picture of elegance in a tight-fitting white dress, with high heels. She has long brunette hair and pale skin. She is holding hands with her grandmother, leading her to the table. The family stand at the table and allow the old woman to choose where she'd like to sit. She chooses the chair beside the window, but does not let go of her granddaughter's hand. The young woman sits beside her. Throughout the dinner, the young woman talks to her grandmother, always making sure her wine glass is full, that she has enough water, that she's happy with her meal. The grandmother positively glows with the attention. I'm so rapt in this spectacle, I don't notice the waitress present me with my dessert.

I've had the pear dish before in Beaune. On that occasion, one fan of sliced pear had been soaked in white wine, the other fan in red. This time, the slices are drowning in a red wine sauce with an island of cassis ice cream in the middle, topped with a dried apple slice.

Perhaps the essence of French cuisine is what they can do with a humble pear. In cooking, a pear transforms into an unctuous, delectable tarte; a perfect partner for goats cheese in puff pastry; and when soaked in wine, it becomes... fruit exceptionnel!

The waitress clears my table and suggests a cafe to finish. Ha! I know better than to ruin a lovely Sunday lunch with French coffee. Without wishing to, I take my leave of this delightful restaurant, and exceptional French cooking, for a year. The journey to Paris is over in two hours. I try not to think of the next twenty-six hours crammed in economy class of a plane. Instead, I think of Craig, back in the barn beside the Loire. I miss him already. Au revoir mon velo!

Made in the USA
Lexington, KY
01 November 2013